Lutheran Dualities

Lutheran Theology
German Perspectives and Positions
Vol. 4

LUTHERISCHER
WELTBUND
**DEUTSCHES
NATIONALKOMITEE**

Lutheran Dualities

Guidance for Preaching the Gospel

Published on behalf of the United Evangelical
Lutheran Church of Germany (VELKD) with the
German National Committee of the Lutheran World
Federation (GNC/LWF) by Christine Axt-Piscalar,
Andreas Ohlemacher and Oliver Schuegraf

Translated by Neville Williamson

EVANGELISCHE VERLAGSANSTALT
Leipzig

Published in German as: Um des Evangeliums willen. Gesetz und Evangelium, Glaube und Werke, Alter und Neuer Bund, Verheißung und Erfüllung. Eine Handreichung für Predigerinnen und Prediger, im Auftrag der Vereinigten Evangelisch-Lutherischen Kirche Deutschlands (VELKD) herausgegeben von Christine Axt-Piscalar und Andreas Ohlemacher, Leipzig 2021.

Bibliographic Information of the German National Library
The German National Library lists this publication in the German National Bibliography; detailed bibliographic data are available on the Internet at http://dnb.de.

© 2022 by Evangelische Verlagsanstalt GmbH · Leipzig
Printed in Germany

This book is printed on age resistant paper.

Cover: Kai-Michael Gustmann, Leipzig
Typesetting: Steffi Glauche, Leipzig
Printing and binding: Hubert & Co., Göttingen

ISBN 978-3-374-07209-5 // eISBN (PDF) 978-3-374-07210-1
www.eva-leipzig.de

Editors' Preface

It has often been noted that the theology of Martin Luther and subsequently Lutheran theology in general are marked by an approach which is reminiscent of the dialectical method. The duality of "law and gospel" might be the most well-known pair. This approach to doing theology is chosen for the sake of the gospel: it can be a help in interpreting the gospel and sharing the Good News of Jesus Christ in the right way. At the same time, Lutheran dualities have been misunderstood or misused in the past and still give rise to questions about meaning and purpose today. However, especially in times when simple answers are often hastily sought, this dialectical approach becomes not only important for preaching but also in theological education. Anne Burghardt, the General Secretary of the Lutheran Word Federation, recently pointed this out:

> "Today, when simplistic answers to complicated questions are widespread, an education that fosters the ability to think in a differentiated way, or even in dialectical categories such as 'law and gospel', 'sinner and righteous at the same time', is extremely important. Simplistic approaches that lead to dividing everything into categories such as 'either/or', 'yes or no', 'right or wrong', without leaving room for discussion and reflection, do not promote dialogue and do not take seriously the complexity of the world around us."*

---

* Anne Burghardt, Address to the Assembly of the German

So how can the Lutheran dualities be applied in an appropriate theological way and thus be useful for Lutheran preaching and teaching? This latest booklet in the series "Lutheran Theology: German Perspectives and Positions" – published by the United Lutheran Church of Germany and the German National Committee of the Lutheran World Federation – wants to offer guidance.

As the name of the booklet series implies, it offers results from German theological research carried out at churches and universities, and directed both towards academic discourse and *praxis pietatis*, in itself a genuine Lutheran concept. Background information might sometimes therefore be necessary to contextualise the topic at hand. This manual „Lutheran dualities: Guidance for preaching the gospel" has been written within a specific German context and with this background it does address a specific reproach. The latter will be explained further at the beginning of the booklet: German theologians using past concepts and phrases that had been misused in an antisemitic way have to decide whether one may continue to make use of these concepts and phrases at all. The historical guilt of the Germans towards people of Jewish religion or connected to Jewish roots obliges them to treat this topic even more sensitively than theologians of other nationalities. In Germany the Jewish-Christian dialogue as an institutionalised format handles these questions in the realm of theology in a most helpful way.

An understanding of the specific German context is necessary in order to avoid ecumenical misunderstandings. One

National Committee of the Lutheran World Federation, 30 November 2021 (manuscript).

chapter heading refers to the "evangelical" way of interpreting the Bible in the church. The term "evangelical" is derived from the Greek word for "gospel", so this indcates that the gospel taught by Jesus Christ is the chosen perspective to read, understand and interpret both New and Old Testament in a Christian way. Other perspectives such as those of other religions, especially Jewish perspectives, as well as historical, literary and other perspectives are certainly also legitimate but are not in the focus of this manual. Churches and theologies in the tradition of the 16th century Reformation do take the gospel as an approach to reading, understanding and interpreting biblical texts. It is important to note that the German word "evangelisch" furthermore indicates plainly the origins in the Reformation period; it is not meant in the more personal or strictly theological sense of the German word "evangelikal", which refers to connotations from other historical developments like the Pietist or charismatic tradition. Unfortunately, in the English-speaking world both those German terms are translated with "evangelical". Therefore, one has to keep in mind that in this manual the term "evangelical" way of interpreting the Bible (in German: "evangelische Art, das Evangelium auszulegen") does address the two layers of meaning of the German word "evangelisch": firstly, in accordance with the gospel, and secondly in the tradition of reformation theology. In Germany, Lutheran, Reformed and United Churches mainly uphold this tradition. It goes without saying that other denominations do read, understand and interpret biblical texts as well both in an "evangelical" and in their own legitimate ways.

For a better understanding it may also be helpful to add a few sentences concerning the denominational landscape in Germany. One main characteristic are the 20 Evangelical regional churches (Landeskirchen). They are territorial churches and are either Lutheran or Reformed by confession, or United (uniert). Roughly a third of the German population belongs to one of those regional churches. All regional churches belong to the Evangelical Church in Germany (EKD) and are thus in communion. Seven Lutheran regional churches form the United Evangelical Lutheran Church of Germany (VELKD). All Lutheran churches are member churches of the Lutheran World Federation to which they relate via the German National Committee of the LWF (GNC/LWF).

Further background information is necessary. Since this manual wants to be of practical use for its readers, considerations are given at the end of each (sub)chapter about those biblical texts suggested for sermons. Lutheran, Reformed, and United churches in Germany do have an order (lectionary) for these biblical texts, called the „Order of Pericopes" (Perikopenordnung). It comprises annual orders of weekly psalms, biblical readings and sermon texts for each Sunday and feast day in the Church year, which are repeated after a period of six years. In former times these orders were binding, nowadays they are a strong suggestion, being at the same time a means of cohesion among the German churches in the reformation tradition. Of course, texts which are not included in these service orders also have to be dealt with carefully to avoid antisemitic strands of interpretation. The focus in this manual is on texts from the German order of pericopes.

Having this background information in mind, the main purpose of the following manual is to show that the lutheran dualities of "law and gospel", "faith and good works", "old and new covenant", and "promise and fulfilment" are still a valid way to open up reading, understanding, and interpretation of biblical texts in an up-to-date fashion. The United Evangelical Church of Germany and the German National Committee of the Lutheran World Federation are convinced that these reflections from a German perspective can be transferred and adopted into other local and regional contexts and therefore hope that they are a helpful and stimulating tool for all those charged with the ministry of preaching and teaching in Lutheran churches worldwide.

Andreas Ohlemacher
Oliver Schuegraf

Foreword

How can preachers cope with the diversity of biblical texts and the great variety of statements they contain, and how can they approach the unity of the Old and New Testaments? In order to understand scripture in its diversity and to interpret its existential meaning, Luther and Lutheran theology make use of contrasting pairs such as law and gospel, faith and works, old and new covenant, promise and fulfilment. The gospel of Jesus Christ serves as a hermeneutical key for the whole of scripture. The interpretation community of the church reads, hears and receives scripture as a whole in the light of the gospel of Jesus Christ, and these pairs – the so-called dualities – are an aid in approaching scripture and revealing its significance for the individual Christian and the congregation. Other approaches to scripture, such as historical-critical exegesis and the Jewish tradition of interpreting the Hebrew Bible, are acknowledged as independent methods and appreciated as an enrichment for the understanding of scripture.

Properly understood, the dualities are not a dead weight dating back to long-gone tradition, but an aid to interpreting the gospel in a way that is relevant to present-day existence and to understanding the specifically Christian use of scripture. This manual aims to make this clear and to whet the appetite of people involved in the ministry of the Word so that they may be prepared to follow the hermeneutical and existential stimulation to which the dualities offer access. At the same time, it is important to keep in mind that the dualities have been and continue to be used falsely in order to propound anti-Jewish stereotypes. By providing information about the meaning and purpose of the dualities, this manual is primarily intended to counteract such opinions. It hopes to give guidance towards a use of the dualities in accordance with the gospel, avoiding every kind of anti-Jewish defamation and debasement. In this sense, it is a response to a request by the Bishops' Conference of the United Evangelical Lutheran Church of Germany (VELKD) from the year 2014 "to reconsider central theological teachings of the Reformation and in so doing not to fall into pejorative stereotypes to the detriment of Judaism". With this request, the Bishops' Conference had reacted to critical discussions about Luther's theology in the Christian-Jewish dialogue which had been increasingly voiced in connection with the Reformation anniversary, and asked the Commission on Theology of the VELKD to clarify the use of dualities in Lutheran theology.

The individual chapters on the respective dualities are of differing character, as can be seen in the length of the chapters, in the respective methodological approach, as well as in the style of argumentation and of writing. This also reflects to some extent the composition of the Commission on Theology, whose members have worked jointly on the manual, bringing in the insights of their various theological disciplines. All kinds of topics were covered: the particular theological importance and the peculiar difficulty of the subject, the different perspectives of the theological disciplines in their approach to the questions dealt with, the focus of the bishops' mandate to develop the dualities in their significance for the Lutheran churches and to present this in such a way that their false use, leading to pejorative stereotypes with regard to Judaism, is thwarted – all these points of view were taken up in a consultation process lasting several years and brought together in the manual.

The diversity of the individual chapters, however, results primarily from the dualities discussed in each case. The duality of law and gospel, for example, with all its theological, hermeneutical, existential and homiletic significance, is treated in much greater detail than the other dualities; this corresponds to the central importance of the distinction between law and gospel in Lutheran theology. The duality of faith and works is presented primarily from a perspective of systematic theology, showing its significance for the life of Christians and their responsibility for the world, and thus emphasising how and to what extent good works are an indispensable part of Christian existence, also in the perspective of Luther and Lutheran theology. In the treatment of the dualities old and new covenant as well as promise and fulfilment, the clarification of exegetical questions plays a much stronger role than in the other chapters. These clarifications of exegesis are to be taken into account for the liturgical use of the dualities in Christian worship – in the celebration of the Lord's Supper and the readings according to the lectionary for the church year. It is particularly important to take exegetical care with these dualities: it helps to ensure that the meaning of the biblical texts is seen in a differentiated way. Thus attention is drawn to how, and how far, the dualities old/new covenant as well as promise/fulfilment make reference to Christ as the specific characteristic of the Christian church, so that Judaism is in no way devalued. In each case, reference to Luther is more or less extensive, depending on what is appropriate. While the duality of law and gospel is typical for Luther, and the contrast between faith and works can also be seen in a specifically

Lutheran light, the dualities old/new covenant as well as promise/fulfilment are not typically Lutheran, but have rather been and are used in various denominations over the course of church history; however, Luther indeed uses these dualities in a special way, in that he sees the gospel of Jesus Christ as formative for determining their relationship.

How these clarifications can be applied in the preparation of sermons is explained in the individual chapters in different ways and with different intensity. Basically, the explanations of the duality of law and gospel form in their entirety a guide towards implementing this duality homiletically. The clarifications on the distinction between the old and the new covenant as well as on faith and works are specifically related to the lectionary texts. In the chapter on the duality of promise and fulfilment, important elements are addressed that play a central role in Christian worship. This duality can primarily be used to open up scope for a creative theological interpretation of biblical texts and intertextualities, especially when the order of service, with its interplay of sermon text and readings, gives opportunity for such creative explanations. The intention is to arouse consciousness and encouragement for such endeavours.

The diversity of the chapters, which has been deliberately retained for this manual, should make a lively impression on the readers providing orientation and at the same time stimulating their own thoughts. The manual clarifies the meaning of the dualities, seeks to elucidate their significance for the interpretation of scripture, unfolds especially the existential significance of the dualities, and helps to grasp the particularity of the Church as an interpretation community in its orientation to the gospel of Jesus Christ. The manual establishes that the correct use of the dualities neither denigrates Judaism nor leads to anti-Jewish dissociation in theology and preaching. The text is a *manual* because it offers help in clarifying these questions. It then lies in the hands of the preachers to conduct the ministry of the Word. They face the challenge of dealing with the diversity of biblical texts and the unity of the Old and New Testaments in such a way that the gospel of Jesus Christ is preached rightly and that Christians can see themselves in the light of that gospel such that they experience the liberating power of the gospel in their lives.

Content

The "evangelical"* way of interpreting the Bible in the church

In order to understand the Bible, it must be interpreted and proclaimed in such a way that it reaches people, enables them to experience God and helps them to experience themselves and the world in the light of the biblical message. All those who are involved in the ministry of the Word are familiar with this challenge. It is not only, but to a large extent, a consequence of the variety of biblical texts in the unity of Old and New Testaments, some of which are felt to be strange or even contradictory. It is a basic task of theology and of the *art of understanding* (hermeneutics) to show how to deal with this appropriately.

The church is an interpretation community in which the Bible as a whole is read, heard, interpreted and appropriated against the background of the gospel of Jesus Christ. This "evangelical way"[1] of reading and proclaiming the Bible in the unity of Old and New Testaments distinguishes the interpretation of the Protestant churches from other approaches to scrip-

---

*   See editors' preface, pp. 6 f.
[1]   The other Christian denominations also interpret scripture against the background of the Christ-event. This manual deals with the specifically Lutheran approach to scripture, here referred to as the "evangelical way" of understanding scripture, because it places the gospel (*Evangelium*) of God's unconditional grace, grasped in faith, at the centre of the interpretation of scripture as a whole.

ture. In its perception of the Old Testament it also differs from the Jewish interpretation of the Hebrew Bible.[2]

It is also distinct from a scientific exegesis that is essentially oriented towards the historical meaning of the texts.[3]

The evangelical way of receiving the Bible in the interpretation community of the church does not level out the diversity and differences of the biblical witness. It does, however, place them against the background of the message of Christ, so that they are understood as derived from and pointing towards that message.

In order to bring the perspective of the gospel of Jesus Christ to bear theologically on scripture in the diversity of its witness and unity as Old and New Testament, Lutheran theology and the church use *hermeneutical dualities*, as they are called in this manual. Dualities here are pairs of theological terms that only unfold their meaning when set in tension with each other. For this manual they are: law and gospel, faith and works, old and new covenant, promise and fulfilment.

---

[2] To emphasise this approach to scripture from the gospel does not imply a devaluation of the Jewish interpretation of the Hebrew Bible. It is an independent way of dealing with the texts of the Jewish tradition and is seen by Christians as such and as an enrichment of scriptural interpretation.

[3] Nevertheless, with regard to historical-critical exegesis it is important to note that its results are to be taken into account and appreciated. The difference between the various approaches to scripture has recently been emphatically underlined by Ingolf Dalferth, who stressed that the perspective of the gospel is hermeneutically fundamental for the Protestant churches; see Ingolf Dalferth, Wirkendes Wort. Bibel, Schrift, Evangelium im Leben der Kirche und der Theologie, Leipzig 2018.

These dualities help to penetrate and systematise theological problems. They are an aid to reading and understanding in order to interpret the Bible and the unity of the Old and New Testaments in the light of the gospel and to develop the significance of the Bible for the self-understanding of the Christian community and the life of faith of the individual.

In this respect the dualities are not to be understood as schematically fixed doctrines, as a reduction of the diversity of scripture or even as a renunciation of certain texts and statements, but as hermeneutical keys that open up the whole of scripture on the basis of the gospel and as an aid to elucidation of God, oneself and the world in contemporary experience. The dualities have to prove their effectivity in these fields, thus revealing their particular importance for preaching.

The Lutheran dualities are subject to strong criticism, especially in the Christian-Jewish dialogue. This criticism is directed at anti-Judaic tendencies which it sees as inevitably associated with the dualities.[4] The use of the Lutheran dualities thus poses a particular challenge: they must be expressed and interpreted in such a way that their significance for the Christian faith is placed in the limelight without allowing room for anti-Judaic tendencies. How is it possible in preaching and teaching to distinguish between the law and the gospel, or any of the other dualities, without falling into anti-Judaic stereotypes or repeating these ill-fated patterns of thought? Above and beyond that, how can one hold fast to the Christian confes-

---

[4] The term *anti-Judaism* is used in what follows to describe stereotypes that may contain a devaluation of Judaism, while the word *anti-Jewish* is used for statements containing polemics directed against Judaism.

sion of faith in Jesus Christ – which stands as a distinction, indeed a contradiction to Jewish belief – yet at the same time hold fast to the indissoluble connection of the Church with the Jewish people and live together in peace and respect for each other? How can the theological use of the Lutheran dualities succeed without leading to a devaluation of the Jewish faith?

This is the task assigned to the Commission on Theology by the Bishops' Conference of the VELKD: to respond to Section 11 of the statement "Luther and the Jews" by the Evangelical Church in Germany (EKD) and to clarify how the challenge described here can be taken up constructively:

> "In theology and church life we face the challenge of rethinking central theological doctrines of the Reformation and of not falling into disparaging anti-Judaic stereotypes. This particularly concerns the distinctions 'law and gospel', 'promise and fulfilment', 'faith and works' and 'old and new covenant'."[5]

The first duality to be clarified here is that of the law and the gospel (1). Afterwards the focus is on the other distinctions, one after the other: faith and works (2.1), old and new covenant (2.2), promise and fulfilment (2.3). It should be borne in mind that these dualities are interrelated: all of them are concerned with the gospel of salvation in Jesus Christ. The guiding principle is the task and the challenge assigned by the

---

[5] EKD-Declaration "Martin Luther and the Jews – a necessary reminder on the occasion of the Reformation anniversary", 11 November 2015 (https://www.ekd.de/en/Martin-Luther-and-the-Jews-272.htm).

bishops as mentioned above. For this reason, the dualities will not be discussed comprehensively in every respect.[6] Rather, the focus lies on their use in worship and on the avoidance of anti-Judaic tendencies. This manual is intended to provide orientation in this regard.

It is necessary to agree in advance on what is meant by anti-Judaic stereotypes and what is to be ruled out when using the dualities: profiling oneself at the expense of another, usually with the aid of a distorted description of their position, so that one's own persuasion appears in a comparatively positive light.

In this sense, this manual is primarily concerned with showing how the aforementioned dualities can be used in preaching without having to resort to a disparaging portrayal of Judaism. It is important to point this out, because in many cases anti-Jewish connotations were attached to the Lutheran dualities. These connotations were frequently to be found in sermons over hundreds of years, and partly even in Luther's own preaching. Whether and to what extent the dualities can also serve to improve mutual understanding in the dialogue between Christianity and Judaism is worth further consideration, but requires a separate presentation.[7]

---

[6] Parallel to this manual, a volume of essays has been published that explores each of the dualities theologically in depth: Die lutherischen Duale Gesetz und Evangelium, Glaube und Werke, Alter und Neuer Bund, Verheißung und Erfüllung, im Auftrag der Vereinigten Evangelisch-Lutherischen Kirche Deutschlands (VELKD), hg. von Christine Axt-Piscalar und Andreas Ohlemacher, Leipzig 2021.

[7] Mutual understanding can only grow in dialogue and in the comparison of Judaism and Christianity, listening to Judaism's own

The avoidance of anti-Judaistic tendencies, however, cannot mean that the confession of Christ is relativised. In confessing Christ as the crucified and resurrected Lord (Rom 10:9), the Church and each individual Christian expresses that conviction which is their only consolation in life and in death. This conviction, which binds the individual to Christ through the action of the Holy Spirit and forms the foundation of his or her whole life, cannot permit any qualification of its confession. Nonetheless, it demands respect for the religious conviction of others. In the interests of the claims to truth made by the Christian and Jewish religions respectively, such respect does not remove the differences but rather testifies and holds to them both – entrusting their eschatological completion to God himself (Rom 11).

---

understanding of concepts such as Torah, law, covenant, works, etc. In this process, attention should not only be paid to the inner diversity and variety of Judaism, but also to the completely different approaches to the questions under discussion here, some of which differ greatly from Christian theology. A further question would be how Judaism itself can be appropriately addressed and presented in a sermon without making overbearing or derogatory statements about the Jewish self-understanding. This question demands separate treatment and is also not to be covered in this manual.

1 Human existence before God: law and gospel[8]

1.1 Law and gospel – "so what?"

It is a common opinion that questions that preoccupied Martin Luther in the 16th century are no longer of interest to people living in the 21st century. In other words: Nowadays people have other problems than the search for a merciful God. Nevertheless, people feel burdened – and in many cases overburdened. They are conscious of their responsibility, which they are not always able to fulfil. Their question is, when is it good enough – and the underlying question is whether they are good enough to stand up to all kinds of judgment, whether internal or external, secular or divine. Or they suddenly come to the realisation that they are not altogether the person they would like to be or should be.

a) Enlightening effect of an old distinction?

Is it possible that precisely for these challenging life situations Luther's distinction between law and gospel can have an enlightening effect, bringing clarification and help? After all, the distinction between law and gospel is the central hermeneutical, theological and homiletic category for Luther and

---

[8]   For a more detailed insight into what follows, cf. Christine Axt-Piscalar, Gesetz und Evangelium. Thesen zur Bedeutung der lutherischen Unterscheidung, in: Die lutherischen Duale (see note 6), pp. 15–48.

Lutheran theology. And its real focus lies on the existential power that opens up people's experience of themselves and the world. If this is the case, this distinction would also have to prove its merit with regard to present-day issues. It would have to open up our own experiences of ourselves and the world, throwing a new light upon them.

Therefore, the purpose of this chapter is to introduce the reader anew to this Lutheran distinction between law and gospel, to open it up in its existentially enlightening power, and to demonstrate how this distinction can be used effectively in preaching, pastoral care and education.

At first glance, however, it would not seem particularly attractive to study the distinction between law and gospel, nor does it appear to be an urgent theological topic. In recent homiletic drafts this distinction does not appear *explicitly.*[9] Students of theology may well judge this topic to be merely of interest in the area of doctrinal history. Pastors may recall more or less heated debates about whether the law or the gospel should correctly be named first – whereby the model of *gospel and law* appears sympathetic, being superficially more charitable. When put the other way round, one may well be reminded of somewhat unpleasant sermons which first bombarded the congregation with the "law" before consoling them with the message of forgiveness for all their sins. The congregation took cover or else hid their embarrassment by letting their thoughts

---

[9] Cf. on the other hand from the perspective of practical theology: Reiner Preul, "Du sollst Evangelium predigen" / "nihil nisi Christus praedicandus" – Gesetz und Evangelium in der Predigt, in: Ulrich Heckel et al. (eds.), Luther heute. Ausstrahlungen der Wittenberger Reformation, Tübingen 2017, pp. 211–229.

wander to distant pleasant pastures; the preacher usually failed at any rate to awaken an existential insight into the damnation of humankind. What, then, is to be gained by reconsidering the distinction between law and gospel?

b) A distinction that helps to reflect

For Luther, this distinction is of the utmost importance. It marks one of those typical *dualities* with which Luther and Lutheran theology seek to bring order, as it were, into theological thought. These dualities are like reading aids with which to view and interpret theological problems, difficult Bible texts, personal faith practice, and church worship.

The first of these dualities which we want to examine particularly closely is the distinction between law and gospel, because that corresponds to Luther's own high regard for it. This distinction helped him to understand the Bible as a whole:

> "And it should be noted that all holy Scripture can be divided into two words, which are commandments or God's laws, and promises and pledges."[10]

Luther also knows that it is not appropriate to look solely for the law in the Old Testament and the gospel in the New Testament. The New Testament is also aware of commandments and proclaims God's will for our life's conduct; while the Old Testament also speaks of God's promise and his mercy:

---

[10] Martin Luther, On the Freedom of a Christian: WA, Vol. 7, p. 23,29 f., Translation at Taylor editions, Oxford University https: //editions.mml.ox.ac.uk/editions/freiheit-1520/.

"There is no book in the Bible in which both are not found; God has always placed them together: the law and the promise."[11]

However, in Luther's opinion, everything we find in the Old as well as in the New Testament is to be read, understood and passed on with a focus on the proclamation of the gospel of Jesus Christ. Thus the Bible is understood in a *Christian* sense. But how does this Christian sense affect the special distinction between law and gospel?

1.2 Law and gospel – the two facets of the Word of God and how they open up our existence

1.2.1 Martin Luther's distinction between law and gospel

For Luther, the essential task of preaching is to interpret the gospel in such a way that it proves itself as a liberating and redeeming power in the lives of the hearers. It is supposed to happen

"in such a way that you hear your God speaking to you."[12]

But what happens when we hear God speaking to us? For Luther it is evident that this affects us in a two-fold manner,

---

[11] Martin Luther, Notes on the Gospel: Third Sunday in Advent (1522): WA, Vol. 10 I 2, pp. 142–180 (edited).

[12] Martin Luther, On the Freedom of a Christian: WA, Vol. 7, p. 22,26, Translation at Taylor editions, Oxford University https://editions.mml.ox.ac.uk/editions/freiheit-1520/.

and that is exactly how we become aware of the existential significance of the distinction between law and gospel.

"One must not preach one thing alone, but rather both words of God."[13]

Luther is convinced that God speaks to us in this *twofold* way – and that this duality should be reflected in the sermon. One form of God's Word, says Luther, is intended to enlighten us about ourselves and lead us to self-knowledge. This is the function of the *law* when it is rightly understood. In another form, the Word of God grants us grace and a new life. This other word is the *gospel of Jesus Christ*.

Within this distinction, a differentiation can be detected. The Word of God in the form of law serves to prepare us for and lead us to the gospel. Why is the Bible sometimes so comforting and then again so harsh? Why can one Bible text fill us at one time with happiness, and with fear and shock at another?

First of all, this distinction can be a help for a Bible reader or a preacher who is sometimes puzzled by the texts. Why does the Bible speak of the love of God which is so strong that not even death or the devil can separate us from it, and then again it speaks of "weeping and gnashing of teeth" (Mt 25:30)? Why do we hear that a person is justified without works, and then again that without works no one may expect to receive a reward before God's throne? Were the authors of the Bible not also aware of such discrepancies? Or is this one of those unresolvable tensions that theologians like to refer to when they

---

[13]   Loc. cit.: WA, Vol. 7, p. 34,11f.

are at a loss, so that we can shrug our shoulders and just carry on?

This is neither one case nor the other! For Luther and Lutheran theology, the distinction between law and gospel offers an aid to reading and understanding that makes these contradictory biblical statements and images of God comprehensible, as well as our ambivalent experiences with the texts of the Bible. God uses these two words in order to have a twofold effect on humans; on the one hand, they reveal human remoteness from God, on the other hand they show God's mercy and kindness.

This antithesis places the distinction between law and gospel in relationship. It helps to make the contradiction understandable as the expression of a common intention: that through the texts people are led to the insight into their lostness (law), so that they can experience the promise of forgiveness as salvation (gospel).

For Luther, the distinction between law and gospel[14] is the *one* great art that makes the theologian a theologian, and that has to be learnt and practised for a lifetime, but is ultimately a gift of God:

"Whoever knows well how to discern the gospel and the law should give thanks to God, and know that he is a theologian."[15]

---

[14] Cf. Oswald Bayer, Martin Luther's Theology, Grand Rapids MI 2008 [based on the German edition: Martin Luthers Theologie. Eine Vergegenwärtigung, Tübingen ³2007], pp. 58–66.

[15] Martin Luther, In epistolam S. Pauli ad Galatas commentariu ([1531] 1535): WA, Vol. 40 I and II, here WA, Vol. 40 I, p. 207,17 f. Translated into English from the German text: D. Martin Luthers

This distinction is for the Reformer "the highest art in Christendom"[16]. Here we are at the centre of Reformation theology. Here we are at the point of decision as to whether Christ is principally an example and an ethical obligation or above all a *gift and reward.* In Luther's understanding, it is the central message of the New Testament to acknowledge this, human salvation accepted in faith: Christ as a gift.[17] 1532, in a New Year's sermon, he formulates what is important to him programmatically:

> "I am going to have these two words unmingled, with each one shown to its own place [...]: the Law for the Old Adam, the Gospel for my timid and terrified conscience."[18]

He who does not properly distinguish between law and gospel will in the end either drive people to despair or lead them to ar-

---

Epistel-Auslegung, Band 4: Der Galaterbrief, ed. by Hermann Kleinknecht, Göttingen ²1987, p. 80.

[16] Martin Luther, "The Distinction between the Law and Gospel," January 1, 1532, Willard Burce, translator, Concordia Journal 18 (April 1992), p. 155.

[17] Cf. esp. Martin Luther, A Brief Instruction on What to Look for and Expect in the Gospels (1521): LW, Vol. 35, pp. 115–129, translated by E. Theodore Bachmann, in: World Wide Wolfmueller, https://wolfmueller.co/martin-luther-on-what-to-look-for-and/.

[18] Martin Luther, "The Distinction between the Law and Gospel," January 1, 1532 (see note 16), p. 162. Luther uses "Old Adam" for people as they live and breathe – sinners for a lifetime. They are so struck by the experience of the law that they despair of themselves, fearing God and fleeing from him.

rogance. In desperation, they would have to realise that they would never be able to be as they should be. Those who are arrogant would assume that they can stand before God by their own efforts – at least better than all the others who do not manage to get that far. The self-imposed pressure would become more and more unbearable. They would be forced to acknowledge that whatever they do, think or say, it is always inadequate.

Rightly understood, the law can confront me with myself in such a way that I can clearly see my own *incurvatio in me ipsum* (my being turned inward on myself) and that I am hopelessly lost. It recalls the scene between Nathan and David, after David's desire for Bathsheba had led him to send her husband Uriah to his death. In the end, David has to acknowledge the truth when the prophet confronts him with himself: "You are the man!" (2 Sam 12:7; cf. from 2 Sam 11) And David recognises it and repents.

The point is that the law, if it is *God's* law, does not remain on external.

"At the same time, I am so convicted at that point [the insight into severe guilt initiated from the outside] that, as David before Nathan, the prophet of God, I can speak my own judgment sentence to myself. The law that accosts me convicts me at the same time, from the inside out; just because it is outside of me does not mean that it is a law that has nothing to do with me, against which I would be nothing but a mechanistic echo; its externity is not a heteronomy."[19]

---

[19]   Oswald Bayer, Martin Luther's Theology (see note 14), p. 61.

God speaks to us through the law and thus enlightens us about ourselves. Luther writes

> "that you hear your God speaking to you, how all your life and works are nothing before God, but that you must, along with everything that is within you, perish forever. When you truly believe this, how you are sinful, then you must despair of yourself."[20]

But in that case something decisive happens:

> "In a way that is quite different from the law, in which God speaks against me, in the gospel he speaks for me."[21]

> "For to preach Christ, and Christ alone, is not to proclaim him as a severe judge who condemns according to the law, but to give expression to the good news of the gospel he has brought."[22]

If the law has provided me with healthy self-knowledge, then the ground is prepared for me to learn how God nevertheless accepts me, without the works of the law, out of pure goodness by faith in the crucified and risen saviour, how he justifies me in his sight, liberates me and declares me to be his child. Because all my guilt is laid upon Christ. Because all Christ's virtue

---

[20] Martin Luther, On the Freedom of a Christian (see note 10): WA, Vol. 7, p. 22,26–29.

[21] Oswald Bayer, Martin Luther's Theology (see note 14), p. 61.

[22] Reiner Preul, "Du sollst Evangelium predigen" / "nihil nisi Christus praedicandus" (see note 9), p. 211.

is laid upon me. Because by faith there is a "joyous exchange"[23]. We are joined to Christ:

> "The faith must be taught aright, by which you are so merged with Christ that you and he become, as it were, one person; you cannot be torn away, but constantly cling to him, saying, I am Christ; and Christ in turn says, I am that sinner who clings to me, and I to him. For we are joined together as one flesh and blood through faith."[24]

Thus the gospel liberates a person from him- or herself, so that they can truly come "into their own", no longer letting their thoughts go round in never-ending circles. These people can stand upright, attentive to God and fellow humans, in the certainty of being loved. They now become humble and strong in equal measure. Humble, knowing by the law that there is no cause to be proud before God and humans. Strong, knowing that they are more deeply comprehended than they could have ever imagined, yet at the same time more deeply loved than they could ever have dreamed. This is roughly what Luther meant with his distinction. To what extent is it relevant for our time and our present-day questions?

---

[23] Cf. Martin Luther, On the Freedom of a Christian (see note 10): WA, Vol. 7, pp. 25,26–26,12.

[24] Martin Luther, In epistolam S. Pauli ad Galatas commentarius (see note 15), pp. 285,24–27; 286,15. Translated into English from the German text: D. Martin Luthers Epistel-Auslegung, Band 4 (see note 15), p. 111.

1.2.2 Understanding from the perspective of systematic theology. What does the distinction between law and gospel achieve?

We put the question once again: why should we continue to deal with this fundamental distinction today? One might see one answer in the prominent position occupied by this duality in Luther's theology; that could at least serve as an impetus to track down the meaning of this duality anew. This topic brings us to the centre of Lutheran thought, which ought to be made clear to today's Christians in its existential significance.

For we are speaking of nothing less than the fact that people's experience of themselves and the world is exposed in its hopelessness (sin) and that the gospel unfolds its liberating power.

To put it in other words: it is precisely this distinction that enlightens us in relation to ourselves. It sheds light on our humanity as presented from the point of view of the Christian faith. It is a process which enlightens a person's true situation (*law*) and leads them to themselves (*gospel*).

When *this* happens, we hear *God* talking to us. It is not a question of a rigid doctrine or simply of an ethical judgement based on commandments. It is a question of a process, initiated by the Word of God, in which a human begins to recognise him- or herself. Humans do not gain such clarity about their situation of their own accord. They need enlightenment. When the enlightenment through the Word of God comes in the form of law, then such insight does not remain on the outside. The awareness is not a foreign body. When the law speaks to a person, it comes from outside, but is then internalised. Suddenly, I see myself as I really am. That means no less than this: I recognise *myself in that which the law reveals about me*. I recognise myself as someone who is not at peace with himself. The misery of humans is that they *hang on to themselves* without being able to truly *come to themselves* in and through their own efforts.

"Wanting in desperation to be oneself" is how the Danish philosopher Søren Kierkegaard describes it.[25]

In a way, this can also take place beyond the Christian message. In the back of our minds, we always have a vague inkling of the *law*. But it is the preaching of the law, through which God's Spirit works upon us and within us, which makes it evident. To be sure, the doctrine of the law is only revealed in its full extent in the context of the gospel; but "existence under the law" is a reality even without the gospel and has always determined our experience of life.[26] The *reality of life* itself serves as our experience of the *law*. This takes place "to some extent wherever, under the pressure of the reality of life, we experience our own inadequacy".[27]

So the law is more than and different from (just) the proclamation of commandments – and the insight that I do not keep them. Just as sin is more than and different from immoral behaviour, so the law uncovers more than my misbehaviour. It exposes my "twisted" being, my *being turned inward on myself*, the *incurvatio in me ipsum*: that we live in a self-centred way, attaching our hearts to the goods of this world and mak-

---

[25] Cf. Sören Kierkegaard, The Sickness unto Death (1849), p. 27.

[26] Cf. Gerhard Ebeling, Dogmatik des christlichen Glaubens, Band 1: Prolegomena. Erster Teil (Der Glaube an Gott den Schöpfer der Welt), Tübingen 1979, p. 261.

[27] Loc. cit., pp. 285 f.

ing ourselves dependent on them; that we allow our lives to be dominated by what is penultimate, so that our actions, thinking and striving are totally pervaded with our self-love, and we forget God, our neighbour, and even ourselves. This is what the law reveals insistently and painfully, as is expressed in Paul's sigh: "Wretched man that I am! Who will rescue me?"[28] In this situation, we encounter God as strange, hidden, and downright hostile to us. The law leads us into existential temptation.

As a consequence, we start to yearn for another life. We start to hope that the good news of grace, the prospect of new life might come true for us. Thus the law creates self-knowledge. The law reveals the split that runs through our life and through us. This is indispensable, because it is we ourselves who stand in the way of our self-knowledge. And it also remains a necessity for the Christian, who is both sinful and righteous[29], and therefore permanently dependent on God's twofold way of speaking. Our inner renewal is so far only a fragment. Or in the stronger language of the "Formula of Concord" (1577):

"For the creature, like a stubborn, recalcitrant donkey, is also still a part of them."[30]

---

[28] Rom 7:24.

[29] Cf. on this: Oswald Bayer, Luther's "simul iustus et peccator": KuD 64, 2018, pp. 249–264.

[30] The Formula of Concord: Solid Declaration (1577), Article VI, 24: The Book of Concord. The Confessions of the Evangelical Lutheran Church, edited by Robert Kolb and Timothy J. Wengert, Minneapolis 2000, p. 591.

By means of this self-knowledge, it becomes clear what the gospel does for us and why it is *good* news. Its redemptive power consists in the fact that we become free from ourselves and thus in truth find ourselves. Luther puts this in a nutshell:

> "In order that you might come out of and away from yourself, i.e. out of your destruction, He put his beloved son Jesus Christ before you and conveys through him His living comforting word: You should give yourself over to him with firm faith and trust in him directly."[31]

We do not lose ourselves thereby, but truly find ourselves. For it is indeed not in ourselves that we find what we are as *persons*, but in the promise of the gospel. In faith, this promise makes us free and determines our existence. And this is nothing less than to receive Christ as a freely offered gift. Everything depends on taking him up in this way – and not just as a model.[32]

Thus the gospel leads people into a freedom won through Christ in faith. It makes them into a new creation (2 Cor 5:17).

In this way the believer also receives the fundamental impulse to live a Christ-like life, marked by love of God, of one's neighbour and creation. It is a life enabled by liberation from one's old self, by the rediscovery and acceptance of one's true self. That is why good works are also essential in the life of

---

[31] Martin Luther, On the Freedom of a Christian: WA, Vol. 7, pp. 22:31–23:1, Translation at Taylor editions, Oxford University (see note 10).

[32] As constantly emphasised in Martin Luther, A Brief Instruction (as note 17).

Christians.[33] Even if good works do not contribute to salvation, the life of love and doing good works are the practical expression of Christians' faith in Christ and of their abiding in the love with which Christ first loved us (1 Jn 4:19).

So for the life of the Christian the Ten Commandments (the Decalogue) serve as orientation for the good order of our own life and of our common world. The law can no longer exclude us from communion with God. Nor does it play any role in our justification, for the gospel is a pure and unconditional gift. Nevertheless, we who remain lifelong sinful and righteous at the same time are dependent on the orientation provided by God's commandments. In the struggle against the Old Adam, that stubborn, recalcitrant donkey mentioned above, the believer will be victorious with the help of the Holy Spirit – and will also suffer setbacks. This remains a lifelong process, in which it also becomes clear that believers cannot gradually achieve emancipation from their neediness or even maintain that the gospel is no longer necessary for them.

1.2.3 Luther's distinction between law and gospel and our preaching

The effect of the law varies, just as sin varies in its manifestations. Preaching is the concrete application of the law to people's present experience of themselves and the world; therein lies the art of preaching with regard to the duality of law and gospel. Accordingly, this is the function of preaching, insofar

---

[33] See section 2.1 of this manual (The distinction between faith and works).

as it has to do with *the law*: it has to "interpret for us", to expose our position "under the law" and thus our existential situation before God. In this respect, the proclamation of the law is in no way determined once and for all. In every new situation, elementary human experiences are described and brought to light through *the law*.

Preachers are bound to avoid three misunderstandings of "preaching the law."

(1) *Law* does not mean that one begins by "thrashing" people and telling them repeatedly that they are lost, only to then comfort them all the more effectively with the gospel.

(2) *Law* does not (only) mean reproaching people for their failure to fulfil moral imperatives.

(3) *Law* does not mean that everything in life goes wrong and that all life in the world without faith looks like hell on earth.

On the contrary, the law is preached in order to enlighten people about themselves, so that they can see themselves better than before – more precisely, in the light of God. This implies that life without God is evidently revealed as a life of alienation and division. Many different themes can illustrate this position *"under the law"*:

– It can naturally be about guilt, about a painful falling short of what I myself recognise as good and right, through my actions or omissions.

– It can be about unmasking false gods, which concerns in a broad sense the transgression of the first commandment:

"Preaching can speak of trust in the true God, but it cannot produce it. Nonetheless it may with some success undermine trust in idolatrous images – in those idols created by false investment of basic trust, by misdirected religious passion for secular values and instances. It can be shown that they are unworthy of basic trust and can ruin human life."[34]

- It can be about understanding how much I live at the expense of others and thereby (voluntarily or involuntarily) exploit, utilise and appropriate them to my advantage.
- It can be about the clarification of processes of "overtribunalisation"[35], meaning that in our time there is a tendency to moralise in the public sphere, passing judgment on everyone who appears before the raised forefinger; whoever fails to live up to the high standards expected is condemned in a disparaging and snobbish fashion.
- It can be about the arrogant and exclusionary view of any form of racism, anti-Judaism and nationalism that devalues others because they are different.
- It can be about the ambivalence of the experience of freedom in the late modern age, which detaches me from all traditions and allows me to shape my life by assessing, rejecting or se-

---

[34] Translated from: Reiner Preul, "Du sollst Evangelium predigen" / "nihil nisi Christus praedicandus" (see note 9), p. 221.

[35] Ulrich H. J. Körtner, Freiheit und Verantwortung. Studien zur Grundlegung theologischer Ethik, Freiburg – Wien ²2010, Band 34, following Odo Marquard, Der angeklagte und der entlastete Mensch in der Philosophie des 18. Jahrhunderts (Lecture in the Herzog-August-Bibliothek in Wolfenbüttel on 23 November 1978): Abschied vom Prinzipiellen. Philosophische Studien, Stuttgart 1981, pp. 39–66, here esp. pp. 47–51.

lecting a variety of options; the drawback is that I am then also solely responsible for success and failure. I am therefore to blame for my own *unlived* life or for the wrong choice, because I once took a *wrong turning* in my life and now can no longer go back.

– It can be about the hubris of humans who want to (and in such a case: must) create themselves by their own efforts. They cannot simply accept, but rather create themselves – or force themselves to do so. In any case, they are desperately thrown back on themselves. At the same time, my ingratitude is made manifest, both in my relationship to God *(vertically)* as well as in the relationship to my fellow humans *(horizontally)* in view of the fact that I always bear the responsibility for myself.

For the sermon, Luther's insight is essential that it is ultimately not the preacher who is able to distinguish between law and gospel and to let them take hold of the human heart, but only the Holy Spirit. God is the "most holy master and teacher" in this matter. This also supersedes Luther's own statement that discernment is the highest art of the theologian.

"The Holy Spirit alone can accomplish this art [...]"[36],

says the reformer – after pondering on the difficulty of making this distinction. Likewise, when a person is struck by the law and comforted by the gospel, it is always an action of the Holy Spirit within the hearer.

---

[36] Both quotations: WA TR, Vol. 2,4, pp. 7–16 (1531: n. 1234).

1.2.4 Consequences for sermon preparation

Luther declares the distinction between law and gospel to be the highest art of theology and thus also of preaching, so that the greatest danger of making mistakes lies just here. Our inner operating system is probably geared more towards the *law* than to the *gospel;* in spite of our correct belief, we do like to trust in our own works.[37] To put it more clearly: we do not always manage to make this necessary and salutary distinction. It makes no difference whether we look at it from the point of view of the preachers who fail to make the right distinction, or else from the perspective of the congregation who fail to distinguish correctly while hearing, so that a false notion arises in their minds: gospel without law, or law without gospel, or even gospel re-shaped by law.[38]

We have now reached the most problematic area of our topic. For it is obviously not that simple with Luther's distinction. Thus, attempts are repeatedly made to reduce or completely deny the importance of the law for the Christian. It is in any case obviously controversial nowadays to see the law as a mirror in which we recognise ourselves as sinners and are made aware of our need for redemption (and therefore also learn to understand the cross). The motto is then: the gospel

---

[37] Cf. Timothy Keller, Center Church: Doing Balanced, Gospel-Centered Ministry in Your City, Grand Rapids 2012, p. 54.

[38] Manfred Josuttis has most explicitly pointed to the risk of preaching legalistically. Cf. ibid. Praxis des Evangeliums zwischen Politik und Religion. Grundprobleme der praktischen Theologie, München ³1983; ibid., Gesetzlichkeit in der Predigt, München ²1969.

alone should be the subject of proclamation and theology. Why do we need the law? Is it not enough to know that God holds his love in store for us, independent of our works? And do we *always* have to see humans as deficient beings? Is that really necessary? Who wants to hear that?

Thus one finds much sympathy for antinomian[39] thinking, i.e. thinking *based on the concept of freedom,* understood as a human property that is intact and good and can be spontaneously put into action. *Being under the law* as a situation of division and alienation recedes into the background against the pathos of this freedom. The law has been overcome:

> "[…] the human being is by nature free, good, and spontaneous. In this sense, the modern age is antinomian."[40]

But then humans are all on their own when it comes to fulfilling this promise of freedom. They must now be what they claim to be, simply by their own efforts and strength. The result is that antinomianism turns into a new nomism.

> "It is of systematic interest that when this lesson was neglected – in a formal sense – the law regularly triumphed. If it was not possible to place the gospel in contrast to the law, then either the gospel itself was understood in the sense of a guideline for correct conduct […] or it even appeared to be superfluous. Speaking in terms of Reformation theology, it was admit-

---

[39] "Nomistic" means *imposing laws and strict rules,* "antinomistic" means the attitude that resists such rules and disputes their sense.

[40] Oswald Bayer, Martin Luther's Theology (see note 14), p. 65.

tedly not the 'law' itself that was recalled to mind. It was rather a certain conception of morality that triumphed – one that began to interpret the nature of Christianity rather than submitting itself to critical scrutiny with respect to the law and the gospel."[41]

In other words, whoever pushes the law out of the front door antinomistically will find that it returns through the back door nomistically, for example as a legalistic interpretation of the gospel.

a. Gospel without law

The gospel becomes banal when it is not related to the existential need of humans, when it is interpreted without any acknowledgement of *being under the law.* It is indeed the case that the existentially enlightening power of the distinction between law and gospel is closely connected to the successful interaction of both: law *and* gospel. If one recognises one's own "being under the law", the liberating and joyful power of the gospel will unfold. Without this self-knowledge it remains a mere message that makes promises whose greatness and significance can hardly be understood. God's action in Christ thus becomes a banality, constantly repeating that God's love is there for us – but we do not find that particularly exciting, nor do we understand why we actually need this love.

---

[41] Translated from: Hans-Martin Barth, Gesetz und Evangelium I: Systematisch-theologisch, in: TRE 13, 1984, pp. 126–142, here p. 130, 9–16.

b. Law without gospel

The reverse case is not one whit better. Here we would be confronted with the law that comes without the gospel – becoming indeed a law unto itself. When the law is active without the gospel and thus legalistic, the negative perception of oneself becomes an end in itself.

The law becomes legalistic when it does not remain related to the gospel. It will possibly encourage a conscious intention towards a moral upgrade, so that after the sermon the hearer goes home believing that it is simply necessary to make more of an effort to meet the demands that are being made – by someone or other. Alternatively, the hearer goes out of the church with a bowed head, because it is abundantly clear that there is no possibility anyway of meeting the requirements.

> "That is why the letters do not enter my heart, but strike me dead."[42]

c. Legalism in preaching: What matters is "that you do not make Christ into a Moses"[43]

Luther's distinction therefore demands that law *and* gospel interact. Where this does not succeed, the law threatens to be-

---

[42] Martin Luther, Sermon on 2 Cor 3:2 ff. on 13th Sunday after Trinity (22 August) 1535 (transcript Georg Rörer): WA, Vol. 41, pp. 411–416, here p. 416,2.

[43] Cf. Martin Luther, A Brief Instruction on What to Look for and Expect in the Gospels: LW, Vol. 35, pp. 115–129 (see note 17), WA, Vol. 10 I 1, pp. 10, 20.

come autonomous. Luther was aware of this danger. He was able to phrase it like this: one should "not make Christ into a Moses." Putting it in this way, Luther criticises all forms of piety, especially the *Christian* ones, as well as all proclamation and theology that do not comprehend the gospel as the message of unconditional grace.

In such a case, Christ is not recognised as a gift, but is merely seen as an ethical model and someone who reminds people to fulfil the divine will (law).[44] In other words: The gospel is good news, not good advice. Luther puts it this way:

> "We preach (to people) not only what they should do, but what God has done for them. [...] Not of our doings do we preach, because we have done nothing. It has been done through Christ."[45]

This is one of Luther's admonitions that we had already taken into consideration: Luther was worried that we might only see Christ as a model for behaviour. That is indeed something which often arouses sympathetic reactions. Jesus is widely appreciated as an exemplary person who was kind to children, treated women fairly, took care of the poor and cured the sick. Jesus was a great sage, whose words teach us how to live a

---

[44] Martin Luther aimed at a form of salvation w*ithin Christianity*, governed by rules; here is an inherent danger of introducing an anti-Judaic undertone that is to be avoided. Luther himself will have seen Judaism in this way.

[45] Martin Luther, Sermon on 2 Cor 3:2 ff. on 15th Sunday after Trinity (5 September) 1535 (transcript Georg Rörer): WA, Vol. 41, pp. 416–422, here p. 422,10.

good life, to love our neighbour and to work for peace and justice. There is nothing to be said against all these statements about Jesus. It is just that Jesus Christ is not first and foremost a role model or a good example. He is first and foremost a gift and blessing to us. Take and eat, receive, believe and breathe again: this is Christ given for you, as it says in the Gospels.[46] Then it is possible to say that the gospel radiates into all areas of life and changes us. But the beginning of all that is good is not what we do, but what we receive. Of course, the gospel urges us to lead a life of love, but the life of love lives from the gospel, which promises grace to the believer and renews the innermost being through the Spirit.

d. Preaching legalism or preaching the law?

If we as preachers do not want to begin with the gospel and yet end up in the law, we have to distinguish between ourselves and the gospel – in order to reassure ourselves. We *are* not gospel. Nor do we *live* the gospel.

In church circles you occasionally hear the saying that we should first be good news before we preach good news, but this is dangerous. If that means to say that our actions should not contradict the gospel, then it has a certain justification. Our lives as individuals and as a congregation should begin to reflect the good that we have received from God. But if this saying implies that our actions themselves could be "gospel", then this is a mistake. That would be a huge overestimation of our

---

[46] Cf. on this: Oswald Bayer, Martin Luther's Theology (see note 14), pp. 58–65.

powers, and we would have fallen into the law. Even if the saying wants to suggest that good deeds alone are sufficient and our words only of secondary importance, then we actually deprive our listeners of what they need.[47] For good deeds in themselves refer only to us and not to Christ. On the other hand, good deeds coupled with good words that speak of Christ not only provide our neighbour with a good example, but also with a gift and a blessing.

> "The chief article and foundation of the gospel is that before you take Christ as an example, you accept and recognise him as a gift, as a present that God has given you and that is your own. This means that when you see or hear of Christ doing or suffering something, you do not doubt that Christ himself, with his deeds and suffering, belongs to you."[48]

It is equally dangerous to preach the gospel re-shaped by law. This means the proclamation of a *conditioned* gospel, one with strings attached. Legalistic preaching is not the preaching of the law. It is the exact opposite.

The preaching of the law makes the gospel shine: "Believe in Christ! Your works will not help you. Nor do they need to, for they cannot do so by any means." Legalistic preaching says the exact opposite: "Yes, you could do something. And you ought to do something, too. It may not be very much, just a lit-

---

[47] See section 2.1 of this manual (The distinction between faith and works).

[48] Martin Luther, A Brief Instruction on What to Look for and Expect in the Gospels: LW, Vol. 35, pp. 115–129 (see note 17).

tle thing, but that is what you could do, should do, and ought to do."

e. Consequences for the grammar and semantics of preaching

Legalistic preaching can also be reflected in grammar: Legalistic preaching is fond of the auxiliary verbs and the conditional mood.

So we "may" in faith do or change this or that, lay emphasis on something or go along with it – but the real message is: Do it, otherwise it will look bad! Or God "would like" (another auxiliary verb!) to do us good, "if only" we would recognise, repent, do good, try harder, witness more boldly, act more lovingly ... . The legalistic sermon imposes certain limits on the unconditionality of grace. Yes indeed, grace, naturally, but then there is a little bit left over: maybe 3 %, or even only 0.1 % – your free will, the correct baptism as an adult, that subtle "If you would only ..." etc. It is always a "mixed calculation", and we humans can certainly only contribute the smaller part, but if we do not do so, then things look bad.

Thus the gospel is legalistic if its validity is supposed to depend on greater or lesser, even minuscule, human precursory acts and contributions. It is the gospel in conditional mood. It is not the *unconditional* promise attached to the simple call to repentance. The grateful consequence is then lost, simply doing good because we feel unconditionally justified. This unconditionality must not be limited by transforming the consequences of justification into conditions of gratitude. This would be an attempt to reinterpret the message of the justification of the sinner, turning it into the requirement that the sinner must now become a better person. Applied to the parable of the prodigal son in Luke 15, that would suggest that the younger son is accepted because he has become a decent person, while the older brother has not yet done so. This is the aberration of reducing the role of the gospel and increasing that of the human, so that in the end it is the human who is most important. Then Christ as *exemplum* (example, model) outshines and surpasses Christ as *sacramentum* (gift of salvation, salvation itself). The idea that we should not believe *in* Jesus, but believe *like* Jesus, tends in the same direction, as does the popular saying that God has no hands or feet but ours. This is legalism. Legalism, on balance, is precisely the refusal to distinguish between law and gospel; it is the permanent confusion of law and gospel.

f. Consequences for structuring the sermon and holding the attention span

Finally, when it comes to planning the structure of a gripping sermon, we should avoid either of two extremes. On the one hand, we might make recourse to a simple sequence of ideas which is used in practically every sermon, in this case by speaking first of the law and then of the gospel. On the other hand, we might well decide to be cautious, having been unsuccessful in the past, and plan to do just the opposite: in this case we would refrain from talking about the listeners' plight before preaching the gospel to them. It is indeed possible to use the contrast between law and gospel to hold people's attention. Then again, the distinction between law and gospel is not supposed to be a definitive sequence (that is to say, in a chronological sense: first one, then the other), but an objective juxtaposition. This can be proved by quoting biblical stories like that of Zacchaeus (Lk 19:1–10), in which the law is not mentioned first at all – but the tax collector whom Jesus visited quickly realised how wrong his life had been as he had lived it until then.

g. The fundamental importance of the duality of law and gospel

With these explanations we wanted to make it clear that the distinction between law and gospel to be found in Luther and Lutheran theology indicates a duality whose significance lies in illuminating the existence of the human being as *being under the law*. This offers help in understanding the manifold snares which hamper human life, revealing them, and leading the listeners to probe into their own existence, as it were, and to enlighten them about themselves and their life. These snares are of many different kinds, and each requires a new interpretation by the preacher based on the situation and experience of the people. The concrete reference to the law when speaking of real-life, present-day existence represents a challenge and demands particular skill in a sermon about the law.

It is clear at the same time that when speaking of the law it is not only and not principally a question of the divine commandments which are broken in human life. It is a question of the manifold pitfalls of life, which the hearers experience as an inhibition, without always being conscious and deeply aware of such inhibitions and their causes.

When dealing with the duality of law and gospel, the aim is not to interpret the gospel legalistically, but to preach Jesus Christ as a gift and the gospel as pure grace. This will bring out the proprium[49] of the gospel and in this way liberate the believer from being under the law. Gospel of Christ means: to proclaim Christ in such a way that a person becomes aware of him- or herself as a recipient.

Combatting all tendencies towards legalism in theology and spirituality, Lutheran theology emphasises the precise distinction between law and gospel in order to preserve the gospel's pure character of grace. This makes it clear that the precise distinction between law and gospel is linked to a theological admonition that is primarily directed *inwardly* – towards Christian preaching and theology – and here, in the context of Christian theology and spirituality, criticises all forms of legalism and legalistic piety for the sake of the gospel. The impetus of this duality of law and gospel – rightly interpreted – is polemically directed inwardly. That is the point of the duality, especially in Luther's own writings.

In its theological, hermeneutical and existential meaning, this duality is in no way influenced by an anti-Judaistic impetus; in other words: the Pharisee is the *Christian* who preaches, teaches and behaves accordingly.[50] This insight into the polemical character of the duality within Christianity is to be taken to heart when it is used. On the whole, given the meaning of the distinction between law and gospel, it is possible to interpret this duality without falling into anti-Judaistic stereotypes.

---

[49] Proprium means here: that which is particular and special in content, sense, and efficacy.

[50] The word "Pharisee", which describes a group in ancient Judaism, is in German usage often associated with a hypocritical attitude. In the sermon, such associations should be handled very carefully.

A polemical estrangement from Judaism, which the Evangelists and Paul – as Jewish Christians – considered theologically necessary in their context, does not exist as a challenge for the Christian congregations today. Here it is necessary to pay attention to the differing contexts of the original Christian congregations and the congregations of the present. While pointing this out, there is no need to relativise the testimony of the gospel of Jesus Christ, which promises salvation in him and grants it by pure grace in faith alone in Jesus Christ, not on the basis of works of the law. This message is to be asserted against *all* forms of relationship to God, to oneself or the world which assume that humans can take themselves and their relationship to God in their own hands. The fact that this is nonetheless repeatedly the case in the context of the Christian churches and among individual Christians reveals that the preaching of the duality of law and gospel is the central hermeneutic key. It serves to bring the gospel of God's unconditional grace to all peoples and thereby to resist the pull towards legalism to which humans, whether intentionally or unintentionally, fall prey. This duality is to be used in Christian preaching in this primarily self-critical way – and not as an anti-Jewish stereotype.

2 The other dualities

In what follows, the other basic Lutheran dualities are discussed: faith and works (cf. 2.1), old and new covenant (cf. 2.2), promise and fulfilment (cf. 2.3).

2.1 The distinction between faith and works[51]

2.1.1 Introductory remarks

Luther's polemic against what he called "works righteousness" forms one basic tenor of his theology. It has therefore often found its way into frequent reiteration of the phrase "works righteousness", which is said to contradict the Reformation understanding of justification by faith. The meaning of "works righteousness" is the attempt by humans to gain merit before God by their own efforts and thus to make a contribution to their salvation. The meaning of *faith*, on the other hand, is the fundamental trust in the gospel's promise of unconditional acceptance by God as a person, even if one's own *works* (thoughts, words, deeds) are to be condemned. "We hold that a person is justified by faith [alone] apart from works prescribed by the law." This Pauline passage (Rom 3:28) serves as

---

[51] Cf. Rochus Leonhardt, Glaube und Werke. Zur Aktualität einer reformatorischen Unterscheidung für die evangelische Ethik, in: Die lutherischen Duale (see note 6), pp. 73–127.

Luther's key biblical evidence for his opinion. In his translation, he added the word "alone", which is not in the original Greek text, to the phrase "by faith", in order to state consistently that the righteousness of God is attained by faith (cf. Rom 1:17). This intensification in Rom 3:28 was also retained in the 2017 revision of the German Luther Bible.

Notwithstanding his harsh criticism of works righteousness and his emphasis on the pure character of grace in the promise of salvation, Luther also emphatically stressed the importance of good works for the life of the Christian. Thus he never denied the necessity of good works in principle and in every respect. On the contrary: he rebuffed the accusation frequently aimed at him, namely that his emphasis on faith would discredit good works, by saying that it was only because of his high esteem for faith that truly good works could come about.

> "Hence it comes that when I exalt faith and reject such works done without faith, they [meaning Luther's opponents of the old faith] accuse me of forbidding good works, when in truth I am trying hard to teach real good works of faith."[52]

Luther's reference to "works done without faith" makes it clear that for him the works of righteousness to which he objects begin at the point where human activities are understood as a contribution to the attainment of grace or to an enhancement of salvation. The following therefore applies to "real good

---

[52] Martin Luther, Treatise on Good Works (1520): LW, Vol. 44, pp. 15-113, Translation at https://www.gutenberg.org/files/418/418-h/418-h.htm.

works of faith": they "must not be carried out in the opinion that through them the person may become righteous before God."[53]

But what is the ruinous effect on human beings of the works righteousness that Luther criticised? And how do good works come to be seen so positively in Lutheran theology that they can be accepted as a proper and indispensable expression of the freedom of the believer? And finally: Can Luther's definition of the relationship between faith and works be described in such a way that it also has something elementary to say to people today?

2.1.2 The decisive point: Relief from the striving for perfection

A clarification of these questions must start from the motive behind Luther's critique of works righteousness. Luther's own experiences are of decisive importance here. On the one hand, he discovered that his dedicated efforts to do thoughts, words and deeds pleasing to God were ultimately motivated by his interest in attaining salvation. But this basically means that good works resulting from the interest in salvation are notoriously determined by self-love and thus by the basic form of sin, egoism. For they are not rooted in devotion to God, but in the ultimately egoistic desire to establish, secure, and increase one's own state of grace. On the other hand, Luther recognised that the all-embracing orientation of the Christian life to God's commandments which would be necessary for the attainment

---

[53] Martin Luther, On the Freedom of a Christian (see note 10): WA, Vol. 7, p. 30,31 f.

of salvation is not possible for any human being. "For," he wrote, "whatever work might be accomplished, there would always remain an anxious doubt whether it pleased God or whether he required something more."[54]

These insights, which grew out of his own practice of piety – that he could not overcome selfishness in the search for salvation and that all his works were imperfect – led Luther to despair and *certainty of condemnation*. To sum up the conclusion of his reflections: if everything depended on the good works of man before God, then all humankind would be given over to damnation. As already indicated above, Luther found the way out of this despair by studying Paul's Epistle to the Romans. He described these events in the well-known account of his conversion, which he included in 1545 in the preface to the Complete Edition of his Latin writings.

While considering the righteousness of God spoken of by Paul in Rom 1:17, Luther "began to understand that the righteousness of God is that by which the righteous lives by a gift of God, namely by faith." Through the gospel of Christ, then, the righteousness of God is revealed, "with which the merciful God justifies us by faith".[55]

This faith is the secure consciousness of the worthiness of salvation given by God – regardless of the imperfection of all

---

[54] Martin Luther, The Bondage of the Will (De servo arbitrio, 1525, WA, Vol. 18, p. 783,26 f.): LW, Vol. 33, pp. 13–294, Translation: Philip S. Watson at https://www.peacebeavercreek.org/uploads/pdf/ bondage-of-the-will.pdf.

[55] Luther, Preface to the Complete Edition of Luther's Latin Writings, Wittenberg, 1545: LW, Vol. 34, pp. 336–337.

human works. It is connected with the relief of the human conscience from the ruinous compulsion previously felt, that one has to contribute to one's own attainment of salvation within the relationship to God.

This compulsion to good works is replaced by the firm confidence that the concern for one's own salvation had been decided by God from the outset – in favour of humans through the life and death of Christ. Since human good works are not decisive in God's sight, the person who trusts in God's mercy finds *assurance of salvation*.

> "Faith is a living, unshakeable confidence in God's grace; [...]. This kind of trust in and knowledge of God's grace makes a person joyful, confident, and happy with regard to God and all creatures. This is what the Holy Spirit does by faith. Through faith, a person will do good to everyone without coercion, willingly and happily; he will serve everyone, suffer everything for the love and praise of God, who has shown him such grace. It is as impossible to separate works from faith as burning and shining from fire."[56]

This quotation elucidates the close connection that exists between faith and works according to Luther. He emphatically criticises good works that are done *in the interests* of salvation, but he is just as insistent that the Christian *assurance* of salva-

---

[56] Luther, Preface to the Epistle of St. Paul to the Romans: LW, Vol. 35, pp. 365–379, Translation: https://www.bestbiblecommentaries.com/.../06/Preface-to-the-Romans-.-Martin-Luther.pdf.

tion is reflected in good works. This happens, as he repeatedly stresses with reference to Mt 7:17 f., as naturally as a good tree bears good fruit.

The way in which good works emerge as a consequence of faith is shown particularly clearly in Luther's interpretation of the Decalogue in the Small Catechism.[57] The formulation "We should fear, love, and trust in God above all things" serves here first of all as an explanation of the first commandment.

Furthermore, the same phrase introduces the interpretation of each of the nine other commandments; these are thus identified as different consequences of trust in God. According to Luther, faith is thus considered the fulfilment of the first commandment; but actions in accordance with the other commandments do not appear of themselves, but only in connection with this faith, as truly good works. They are therefore pleasing to God only and precisely when they "receive from it [i.e. faith] the inflow of their goodness, like a loan."[58]

Good works are no longer regarded as a prerequisite for certainty of salvation in the faith, but as its factually indispensable consequence, even though no longer decisive for salvation. As a tangible result, the addressee of Christian activities is not God but our neighbour.

Because Christians now know that they neither can nor must attain their own merits before *God*, they direct their "ethical energies", and loving Christian perception, completely to-

---

[57] Martin Luther, Small Catechism: The Book of Concord (see note 30), pp. 345–375.

[58] Martin Luther, Treatise on Good Works (1520): LW, Vol. 44, pp. 15–113 (see note 52).

wards the *neighbours*. Meeting their needs is for believers an imperative rooted in gratitude:

> "And although [Christians] are now completely free, they should make themselves into a willing servant in order to help their neighbour, [...] and behave and treat their neighbour as God has treated them through Christ. [...] For just as our neighbour suffers want and needs to partake in our abundance, so it was with us when we suffered want before God and were in need of His grace. Therefore, just as God helped us without reward through Christ, so we should through our body and its works do nothing other than help our neighbour."[59]

This orientation of the good works of the believer towards the neighbour led Luther to focus on the secular social structures of life as a field where Christian love could be put into action. The now obsolete ideology of works righteousness had assumed that one would come closest to the desired ideal of perfection by withdrawing from the sin-laden world into monastic existence. On the contrary, says Luther, the Christian life does not become reality when the believer performs something *out of the ordinary*, but when faith proves its worth in the utterly *ordinary* structures of life in this world.

He assumes, in fact, "that the Christian finds himself in a certain trade and position set by God, and that it is his task to lead his Christian life in precisely this trade and position. [...] God does not want particularly good works, but simple every-

---

[59] Martin Luther, On the Freedom of a Christian (see note 10): WA, Vol. 7, pp. 35:25–27; 36:4–8.

day obedience, which is carried out in the same way in the various different contexts of life in which the individual is placed."[60]

Apart from the integration of Christian action into the areas of responsibility of human life described above, Luther also knows of other ways in which neighbourly love can be put into practice. First of all, there is "unbound love of one's neighbour",[61] a form of Christian action "that follows the precepts of the Sermon on the Mount and culminates in the renunciation of one's own rights and possessions".[62] In addition, in Luther's "ethics of Christian freedom"[63], the abstract validity of moral norms can be less important than behaviour which is guided by the commandment to love and is appropriate to the situation. The guiding principle here is that the Christian is freed to act spontaneously in faith. This makes it possible to do what is good for the specific neighbour in the respective situation without being bound to predefined normative instances. Even the validity of the Decalogue can be relativised as far as the literal rules it contains are concerned. Luther himself expresses this possibility of unbound love of one's neighbour by referring to 1 Sam 10:6 f. and Rom 8:2 as follows: "A Christian who

[60] Translated from: Andreas Stegmann, Luthers Auffassung vom christlichen Leben, Tübingen 2014 (BHTh 175), pp. 374 f.

[61] Cf. Reinhard Schwarz, Martin Luther. Lehrer der christlichen Religion, Tübingen ²2016, pp. 430 ff.

[62] Loc. cit., p. 442.

[63] Gerhard Ebeling, Luthers Kampf gegen die Moralisierung des Christlichen (1983), in: id., Lutherstudien III. Begriffsuntersuchungen – Textinterpretationen – Wirkungsgeschichtliches, Tübingen 1985, pp. 44–73, here p. 71.

lives in this faith has no need of a teacher of good works, but whatever he finds to do he does, and all is well done."[64]

In any case, it is love that guides the Christian – whether doing service in structures of worldly life, renouncing selfish demands or spontaneously helping the neighbours in their concrete situation and needs. For Luther, the fundamental impulse for this love comes from faith in Christ and the experience of the love with which God first loved us (1 John 4:19). This leads believers to look beyond themselves, so that they can "serve, help, and do everything for their neighbour, just as they see God has done and does with them through Christ."[65]

According to Luther, however, the practice of Christian charity in the secular world will never lead to a perfect (sinless) overall situation. The good works of the believer will always be subject to that insurmountable imperfection that characterises the sinful creation. This means that the works of the Christian believer are never free from moral ambivalence. Luther himself expresses this moral ambivalence. He holds (following Ps 143:2b) that the Christian must "entirely despair of his works, believing that they cannot be good" and are merely "without guilt and are good, not by their own nature, but by the mercy and grace of God. [...] Therefore we must fear because of the works, but comfort ourselves because of the grace of God."[66] Thus it is also true for the freedom of

---

[64] Martin Luther, On Good Works: LW, Vol. 44, pp. 15–113 (see note 52), WA, Vol. 6, p. 207,4f.

[65] Martin Luther, The Freedom of a Christian (1520), (see note 10).

[66] Martin Luther, Treatise on Good Works (1520): LW, Vol. 44, pp. 15–113 (see note 52), WA, Vol. 6, pp. 215.32f.; 216.3–6.

the Christian "that no man can succeed in exerting it fault-lessly."[67]

This indicates how Luther's definition of the relationship between faith and works is relevant today:

– On the one hand, his *critique of works righteousness* can be reformulated as a rejection of an exaggerated *world-improvement activism*. This refers to an attitude according to which certain moral and/or political convictions as well as orientations for action are given quasi-statutory status, ruling out alternatives for Christians. Luther's critique, on the other hand, places human action in the realm of the penultimate; this puts it into salutary relationship to its own high expectations – salutary because the involvement of Christians in the secular world no longer demands that they bring about God's kingdom on earth by their own efforts.
– Luther's *emphasis on the necessity of good works,* on the other hand, contrasts with the view according to which the point of the Christian life is *quietistic passivity* – remaining subordinate to life structures that are supposedly immutable.

Faith in the tradition of the Reformation, on the other hand, aims decidedly at involvement in the secular world and at the active assumption of responsibility in the worldly structures of life. Because the role played by good works in the relationship with God is not decisive for salvation, the historical reality on

---

[67] Wolfgang Huber, Glaubensfragen. Eine evangelische Orientierung, Munich 2017, p. 122.

earth is the field of activity for Christian charity. This takes place in such a way that the commitment to the welfare of the neighbour is tied to awareness of the moral ambivalence of all human activity.

2.1.3 Consequences for sermon preparation

Understood in this way, the sense of the Lutheran duality of faith and works also opens up perspectives for structuring sermons. It should be noted that the relationship between the two was not defined by the Reformation with an anti-Judaistic tendency. For it is about the relationship between the *person* of a human on the one hand and the sum of their *works* (deeds and misdeeds) on the other hand when it comes to the relationship with God and about how this is expressed in the context of *Christian* theology and spiritual culture. From this point of view, it is important not to assign to Judaism a path to salvation "based on works", but to understand the duality with regard to forms of *inner-Christian* spiritual practice and theology. These do not correspond to the gospel as long as they make a person's standing before God dependent on the doing of good works. Luther's criticism of works righteousness, by the way, was principally directed at his Christian opponents – those who adhered to the old faith as well as the "enthusiasts". The duality of faith and works should therefore apply to *any* manifestation of the human relationship to God that conceives the person from their deeds and misdeeds and rates the right relationship to God on this basis. By liberating humans from this tendency to identify the person with their works, the duality is intended to criticise that basic existential situation in which people's self-perception depends on what they achieve and their standing in the world is determined by what they have made of themselves.

The Lutheran rejection of exaggerated world-improvement activism mentioned above can be seen as a contemporary starting point for a modern gospel-grounded sermon on the relationship between faith and works, should the distinction between God's action and human action not be sufficiently emphasised. This is, of course, not foreign to the *social-ethical* attitude within some sections of modern German Protestantism. In this case, it must be made evident that works are connected with faith, i.e. the trust in the fact that the existence of reality does not depend on human actions.

In addition, there are tendencies to limit the legitimate diversity of actions performed in faith and to narrow down ethically controversial issues to a single supposedly legitimate point of view. This entails the risk that certain morally founded political options for action are theologically enhanced and thereby excluded from factual criticism. This also tends to undermine the plurality of opinions in issues of penultimate significance, something which is highly important for the Protestant religious culture. If this is counteracted in church sermons, the original intention of the Lutheran duality of faith and works can gain topicality. Part of this distinction focusses on the fact that faith unselfishly supports the neighbour, our common planet and its welfare. But it is not necessarily so that the believers and the church automatically recognise what is good for our neighbour in each individual case, or what exactly promotes the good of the world; they do not know it better than all the others, but are also called to struggle for the answers in a process of debate. This means first of all that in dealing with such questions faith has to consider positions outside the church, come to an understanding with them and cooperate with their proponents. Secondly, it means that official church statements in such cases, just like the decisions of individual Christians, have to be made to the best of their knowledge and belief, but in the awareness of possible error and later correction – which in principle allows room for a variety of possible answers. An important limitation of this variety, however, is the knowledge of God's love for all people, as proclaimed by the gospel.

There is a further point – more in the realm of *individual ethics* – at which the gospel-grounded sermon can bring the Lutheran distinction between faith and works to bear today. This concerns the experience of stress and overburdening suffered by many people. Such experiences of suffering are particularly common where people feel compelled – or indeed force themselves – to meet all the demands of professional and private life as well as possible. The promise given by the gospel and proclaimed in the sermon, that every person who believes is unconditionally accepted by God, can help to break the vicious circle of this compulsion to optimise one's life. This creates a liberating distance to those demands of life which people fail to fulfil comprehensively over and over again. Through the freedom thus gained, the human being is no longer obliged to form his or her person by their own actions. On the other hand, this same freedom motivates one to do those good works which Luther demanded as indispensable consequences of faith. These works of Christian charity are to be done to the best of one's knowledge and belief, regardless of the fact that they do not make a person better or worse before God – admittedly always in the awareness of their insurmountable moral ambivalence. Where this truth is proclaimed in the church, the heart of the message of justification by faith is interpreted in such a way that the works of a Christian are clearly shown to be a consequence of the specifically Christian freedom.

2.1.4 Consequences for structuring the sermon

The freedom of the Christian comes to fruition, as it were, in the good works of the believer. This can also come to be expressed theologically in the combination of liturgical texts proposed for the worship services. Take for example the 18th Sunday after Trinity in the new lectionary for Evangelical churches in Germany*, James 2:14–28, which is included as the sermon text for the first series of service orders, contains the following key sentences, which may well be clearly disconcerting, given the explanations in the last section:

> "What good is it, my brothers and sisters, if you say you have faith but do not have works? Can faith save you? [...] So faith by itself, if it has no works, is dead. [...] For just as the body without the spirit is dead, so faith without works is also dead."

However, if the texts proposed for this Sunday are not taken individually, but are set in relation to one another, a "network" emerges which brings out the Sunday theme in the sense of what has been developed above:

– The motto for the week ahead, which is quoted in the greeting at the beginning of the service, sets the tone: "The com-

---

* See editors' preface, p. 8, with regard to the lectionary.

mandment we have from him is this: those who love God must love their brothers and sisters also" (1 Jn 4:21).

– The Psalm for the week (Ps 1: The Two Ways), with its image of the tree planted by the water which yields its fruit in its season, leads us poetically to the idea of growth, encouraged by the desire to immerse oneself in the law, not out of duty, but with heart and soul (and love).

– The Old Testament reading (Ex 20:1–17) then brings the Ten Commandments into play, but with a narrative framework and Moses' decisive interpretation: "Do not be afraid!"

– The epistle (Eph 5:15–20) takes up the trail laid by the psalm
  • action as the fruit of trust in God: "Live as children of light
  • for the fruit of the light is found in all that is good and right and true." (Verses 8–9).

– The Gospel, finally, brings the narrative of Jesus' encounter with the rich man in the version of Mark's Gospel (Mk 10:17–27). This intensifies the severity of God's demands so radically that even the disciples are astounded and ask themselves, "Who can then be saved?" The story then ends when Jesus says, "For mortals it is impossible, but not for God; for God all things are possible."

Thus the new lectionary offers a textual panorama which opens up room for a sermon on the "epistle of straw" (as Luther apostrophised the Epistle of James).[68] It can be heard and interpreted as a text that teaches us to understand the good works of a Christian as the fruit of trust in God's liberating

---

[68] Martin Luther, Preface to the New Testament (1522), WA, Vol. DB 6; p. 10,33 f.).

promise of salvation and thus makes it clear that "it is impossible to separate works from faith."[69]

Above and beyond that, these texts must be seen in the broader context of the service as a whole. For example, the German hymn suggested for the week expands and deepens the reflection on the connection between faith and works on this 18th Sunday after Trinity:

> "Give my faith, courage and strength, and let it be active in love, that by its fruits one may know that it is not a vain dream and a false facade [...] (EG 414).[70]

---

[69] See quotation of note 56.

[70] The texts for Reformation Day present a similar case. James 2:14–18,26 is also proposed in a somewhat shorter but more pointed form as an auxiliary text among those suggested for this day: Rom 3:21–28; Gal 5:1–6; the Beatitudes in Mt 5 and the plea for freedom from fear: "Do not be afraid; you are of more value than [...]" in Mt 10. The motto for the week from 1 Cor 3:11 sums it up: "No one can lay any foundation other than the one that has been laid; that foundation is Jesus Christ." Here, too, the hymn for the week, Luther's ballad of the rescue of a prisoner from the devil, may add another dimension to the room for interpretation given by the texts: "Dear Christians, One and All, Rejoice". – If we go through all the Sundays in the church year, there are always opportunities to develop and illustrate the connection between faith and works with the help of hymns, e. g. (as the final example) at the 20th Sunday after Trinity by the hymn "Wohl denen, die da wandeln".

2.2 The distinction between the old and new covenant[71]

2.2.1 Introductory remarks

The distinction between the old and new covenants is found in Martin Luther's writings,[72] but it was not "invented" by him, as it were; it is not a decidedly Lutheran distinction such as the duality of law and gospel. Luther uses the scriptural expression, but does not attach particular prominence to the explicit distinction between old and new covenants.

However, especially in his late period, the Reformer introduced into this distinction a theologically fatal devaluation of God's people Israel – with highly problematic statements about the Jews. Therefore it is necessary to ask critically: Is the distinction between the old and new covenants directed against Israel? Does it therefore encourage anti-Judaic polemics? In order to deal with these questions, we are not going to examine Luther's statements directly, but we discuss the exegetical findings in order to draw attention to differentiations that must be respected for a theological understanding of this distinction. Before we do this, we should emphasise the fundamental sig-

---

[71] Cf. Ulrich Heckel, Alter und neuer Bund. Zur Bedeutung dieses Gegensatzes in der biblischen Überlieferung, in: Die lutherischen Duale (see note 6), pp. 151–232.

[72] Cf. Martin Luther, Second Preface to the Prophet Ezekiel (1541): LW, Vol. 35, pp. 283–292, WA, Vol. DB 11 I, pp. 398–403. In his Bible translation (1545) Luther speaks of the "new covenant" only in Jer 31:31, and only uses the word "covenant" in the New Testament in Rom 9:4; otherwise he translates "testament" in all cases, for example in all four accounts of the Lord's Supper "new testament" (Mt 26:28; Mk 14:24; Lk 22:20; 1 Cor 11:25).

nificance of the expression "new covenant" in the worship of the Christian churches, which makes theological reflection on the mention of new and old covenant necessary: it has its primary place in the celebration of the Lord's Supper. The words of institution explicitly speak of the new covenant, which was established through Jesus' death on the cross and which all those taking part in the Lord's Supper enter into. Because the discourse on the new covenant is anchored in the tradition of the Lord's Supper, it has a highly prominent position for the Christian community. It expresses the particular significance of Jesus' death on the cross for our salvation, and it shapes the understanding of those who by faith have fellowship with the crucified and risen Christ and with one another.

It is precisely on account of this central and inalienable significance for church worship that we must give meticulous attention to the relationship between the announcement of the new covenant and the understanding of the old covenant, and to the possibility that speaking of the new covenant involves an anti-Judaistic tendency.

2.2.2 The promise of a new covenant in the Old Testament

In searching for the origin of the old and new covenant distinction, we come across Jer 31:31–34:

> "The days are surely coming, says the Lord, when I will make a new covenant with the house of Israel and the house of Judah. It will not be like the covenant that I made with their ancestors when I took them by the hand to bring them out of the land of Egypt—a covenant that they broke, though I was their husband, says the Lord. But this is the covenant that I will make with the

house of Israel after those days, says the Lord: I will put my law within them, and I will write it on their hearts; and I will be their God, and they shall be my people. No longer shall they teach one another, or say to each other, 'Know the Lord', for they shall all know me, from the least of them to the greatest, says the Lord; for I will forgive their iniquity, and remember their sin no more."

In this passage the new covenant is announced, and the difference is named straight away: "not like the covenant that I made with their ancestors", namely at Sinai (cf. Ex 24).

It is telling that the contrast is formulated within the Old Testament and is therefore not a Christian invention. The old covenant is old, because it was broken – for which the story of the Golden Calf stands (Ex 32). The new covenant is new because it makes something new out of Israel and Judah. God forgives the breach of the covenant and brings about a fundamental, even creative renewal of the people. Henceforth the will of God is written in the hearts of the people as Torah. It is no longer written outwardly on tablets of stone; it has been turned, so to speak, into flesh and blood.[73] Already here, in

---

[73] Cf. Ezekiel 11:19–20: "I will give them one heart, and put a new spirit within them; I will remove the heart of stone from their flesh and give them a heart of flesh, so that they may follow my statutes and keep my ordinances and obey them. Then they shall be my people, and I will be their God." – Cf. also in the form of an intercession Ps 51:12–14: "Create in me a clean heart, O God, and put a new and right spirit within me. Do not cast me away from your presence, and do not take your holy spirit from me. Restore to me the joy of your salvation, and sustain in me a willing spirit."

post-exilic times, proclaimed by an Old Testament prophet, a new covenant is envisaged – for the people of God and not against them.

Such mention of the *new covenant* was not explicitly received within the Old Testament, even though the *establishment of the covenant* is used in (post-)exilic priestly texts of the Pentateuch, following the direction set by the Jeremiah text with its emphasis on God's sovereign action. In Judaism, too, this line is pursued in terms of theological content, but not for the purpose of terminology. Here, the *twofold conclusion* of the Old Testament becomes recognisable in the reception of Judaism and Christianity.[74]

2.2.3 Reference to the new covenant in the New Testament, especially in the tradition of the Last Supper of Jesus

The term "new covenant" is then also found in the New Testament. Mark and Matthew speak of the blood of the covenant in the context of Jesus' last meal (Mk 14:24; Mt 26:28), alluding to Ex 24:8. Luke and Paul speak explicitly of the new covenant in the same context:

"And [Jesus] did the same with the cup after supper, saying, 'This cup that is poured out for you is the new covenant in my blood'." (Lk 22:20)

"In the same way he took the cup also, after supper, saying, 'This cup is the new covenant in my blood. Do this, as often as you drink it, in remembrance of me'." (1 Cor. 11:25)

---

[74] Cf. section 2.3 of this manual (The distinction between promise and fulfilment), especially 2.3.7.

In any case they are different covenants: there the covenant of Sinai, here the salvation brought by the death of Jesus. Mark and Matthew compare the blood sprinkled by Moses to the blood that Jesus shed for the forgiveness of sins. Luke and Paul interpret the words spoken over the cup in the sense of the new covenant made for the forgiveness of sins, as in Jer 31:31–34 quoted above, and now instituted by Jesus. It is in this sense that the reference to the new covenant has been incorporated into the communion tradition of the Protestant churches. If Jesus has made a new covenant in the Lord's Supper through his vicarious death, then the question arises, what has become of God's covenant with Israel?

2.2.4 The new covenant and the permanent election of Israel

The question of the covenant with Israel is particularly sensitive, because the use of the expression "new covenant" in the church tradition was often directed against Israel in an anti-Judaistic way, as if God's covenant with his people was finished and the Church had taken the place of Israel. When Paul speaks of the new covenant, though, it does not mean that the new covenant established by Jesus' death on the cross renders the covenant with Israel invalid, as we can see in what follows. That is why present-day Christians are faced with the challenge of harmonising the concept of Israel's lasting election today with the factual existence of two religions. This challenge for thinking and faith can ultimately only be resolved at the eschaton, the end and goal of all time, long hoped-for and to be brought about by God.

In the face of this challenge, there are differing interpretations of Rom 9–11. Some exegetes emphasise that with the new covenant established by the death of Jesus on the cross, the previous Sinai covenant as a sign of election has not lapsed, but remains an expression of God's faithfulness to Israel. Others assume that the promise of a new covenant has been fulfilled in Christ and that the previous covenant of Sinai has become an old covenant, temporarily put aside. That all Israel will be saved is undisputed for both sides, but they do not agree as to whether God or Christ is meant by the Deliverer out of Zion (11:26). Finally, there is a third group which understands God's covenant with Israel to be primarily derived from the covenant with Abraham, based on God's *promise* and accepted by *faith*; Abraham and the "cloud of witnesses" (cf. Heb 11) in the Old Testament believed God's promise (cf. Rom 9; Gal 3) and the evidence of his righteousness, which is already a promise in expectation of Christ and became reality in Jesus Christ, who is therefore also the Deliverer out of Zion at the end of time.

Therefore, in view of Rom 9–11, it is necessary to clarify which covenants and which promises Paul was referring to.

According to Rom 9–11, the covenants and the law and the promises belong to the signs of Israel's enduring election (Rom 9:4,6–13; 11:5,28; cf. Eph 2:12). God's word has not failed (Rom 9:6). God has not rejected his people (11:1). God's gifts of grace (here: of covenant and promises) are irrevocable (Rom 11:29; cf. 9:4,8f.; 11:27). Ultimately, the hope of salvation of *all* Israel is founded on the promise of an eschatological covenant that consists in the forgiveness of sins (11:27), as already promised by the new covenant of Jer 31:31,34.

Paul goes on to make a distinction in Rom 9–11 as well as in Galatians (Gal 3:6–4:31) between two kinds of descendants of Abraham. Not all who come from Israel *belong* to Israel (Rom

9:6). All Israelites are children of the flesh (9:8), that is, descendants in the flesh from Abraham as their ancestor according to the flesh (4:1). But not all are children of the promise. According to Paul, only the spiritual descendants in faith (4:11f.; 9:8) belong to them, i. e., Jewish Christians baptised into Christ, the *one* offspring of Abraham (Gal. 3:7f.,16,27,29). This remnant that will be saved (Rom 9:27; 11:5), i.e. the existence of the Jewish Christians, is for Paul the visible proof that God is faithful to his word (9:6) and holds fast to his election (11,5). "But not all," that is, only a few, "have obeyed the good news" (10:16). "The rest" who have not come to faith in Christ have been hardened by God (11:7 passivum divinum). This hardening, however, happened only to a part of Israel, and that only for a limited time (11:25). For when the full number of the Gentiles has attained salvation, then at the end of time Christ will come out of Zion as the Deliverer and, for the salvation of all Israel, will complete the forgiveness that was promised with the new covenant in Jer 31:31–34.[75] Then, along with *all Israel*, the Jewish descendants of Abraham will also attain the righteousness reckoned by God to everyone who believes in the gospel of Christ (Rom 1:16f.; 3:21–26; 4; 10:3f.; Gal 3:6–8).

This gospel of righteousness through Christ is the end of the law (Rom 10:3f.). For Paul this sets aside not only the Torah but also the covenant of Sinai (Gal 3:17,23–25; 4,24f.), making the Sinai covenant into the old covenant (2 Cor 3:14).

It is the *promises* that remain valid from the covenants. Therefore the concept of covenant must not be reduced to the Sinai covenant with the Torah, but Paul speaks in Rom 9:4 of

---

[75] Rom 11:25–27; cf. Isa 59:20f.; 1 Th 1:10; Phil 3:20; Gal 4:26.

"covenants" in the plural and thus includes – which is often overlooked – also and particularly the promises, analogous to the "two covenants" in Gal 4:24. These include the Messianic prophecies (Rom 1:2;15:12, quoting Isa 11:10), the promises to the fathers, especially Abraham (Gal 3:6–4:31; Rom 4; 9:4f,7f.; 15:8), and the proclamation of forgiveness through a new covenant with Israel (Jer 31:31–34; 1 Cor 11:24f.; 2 Cor 3:6; Rom 11:26f.).

All these promises are scriptural passages that we read today as independent texts in their original meaning and historical context. In the literal sense, there is no mention of Jesus Christ. But then, after Jesus' appearance, Paul interprets them from a Christian perspective; since they have been fulfilled in Christ, he understands them to have referred to Christ (Gal 3:16; Rom 1:1–3; 2 Cor 1:18,20). According to this view, the prophets had already promised the gospel of the righteousness of God in the Holy Scriptures beforehand (Rom 1:1f.); it had been attested by the law and the prophets (Rom 3:21) – by the Pentateuch through the promise to Abraham (Rom 4:.13–25; Gal 3:6–8,18), by the prophets in their messianic (Rom 15:12) and eschatological predictions (Rom 9:27f.; 11:26f.). In all this, God is the actual author who speaks through the prophets (Rom 1:1f.).

All these promises to the fathers (Rom 15:8; cf. 9:4f.,8f.; 11:26–28) retain their validity. With this the covenant of commitment has lost its relevance, but not the covenant of promise. That covenant remains for Paul an expression of God's faithfulness to His promises to Israel. *God's faithfulness to the covenant consists in his faithfulness to the promise*: when Christ comes out of Zion as a redeemer at the end of time, then all Israel will be saved, as promised by the prophets (11:26).

Then the distinction between the two kinds of Israel (9:6) will be abolished, the separation between Jewish Christians and the rest of Abraham's descendants who do not believe in Christ will finally be overcome, and the unity of all Israel will be complete. Thus it is finally clear

> "that Paul did not expect that non-Christian Jews would come to be included in the redemption of all Israel by some special provision avoiding the path to salvation by faith in Christ," but "that God would lead the non-Christian majority of Israel to salvation by leading them onto the path of faith in Christ."[76]

The conclusion from this is as follows: Christians and Jews differ from one another at present because of the confession of Jesus Christ. According to Paul, it is the purpose of God that there is an Israel that does not believe in Jesus Christ as the Messiah. In this way, God realises his plan of salvation until all Gentiles will have entered into the covenant of promise realised in Christ and then, according to God's will, all Israel will also be saved. Thus today two religions stand opposite each other, each of which is to be respected in its independence. For Christians, this respect is based on the recognition of God's plan of salvation, which does not foresee an Israel that believes in Christ until all Gentiles are brought into the covenant of promise. This respect for God's plan of salvation forbids any attempt to convert Israel that goes beyond the general proclamation of the gospel to all the world. And it is supported by the

---

[76] Translated from Michael Wolter, Der Brief an die Römer (EKK VI/1-2), Neukirchen-Vluyn et al. 2014–2019, Vol. 2, pp. 215.225.

apostle's admonition not to be boastful (Rom 11:17f.) as those whom God has taken into the covenant of promise by pure grace. With Israel, Christians hope for the eschatological realisation of God's counsel and his all-encompassing salvation. God's faithfulness to the covenant is according to Paul his faithfulness to the promise. In Christ, God has confirmed the promises to the fathers (Rom 15:8). He will complete his covenant promises of salvation to *all Israel* when Christ (Hebrew: Meshiach = the anointed one) will come out of Zion as Deliverer at his second coming (11:26). Until then the Christian Church and Israel will have to endure the tension of existing alongside one another as different religions, but at the end of time both can await God's redemption, who has chosen Israel, remains faithful to his promises in Christ and will finally be merciful to all (11:32).

2.2.5 Ministers of the new covenant

Another statement that Paul makes in 2 Cor 3:4–18 is significant for our context:

> "Such is the confidence that we have through Christ towards God. Not that we are competent of ourselves to claim anything as coming from us; our competence is from God, who has made us competent to be ministers of a new covenant, not of letter but of spirit; for the letter kills, but the Spirit gives life. […] But their minds were hardened. Indeed, to this very day, when they hear the reading of the old covenant, that same veil is still there, since only in Christ is it set aside."

Here it is also clear that Paul is not comparing two epochs (then and now), but rather law with the gospel, the ministry of Moses with his own as an apostle, the Torah of Sinai with the Spirit of Christ. He is speaking of a difference related to salvation and the path leading to it, a soteriological difference. Paul defends himself against attacks coming from his (Jewish-) Christian opponents. In spite of all his criticism of the Torah, Paul is not engaged in anti-Jewish polemics, but primarily in an internal Christian controversy within the church of Corinth. He describes the contrast between the old covenant and the gospel, which is not a new Torah to supersede the old one and thus demands obedience. He emphasises that the Torah, as interpreted by his inner-Christian opponents, does not give life or righteousness, but rather serves death and condemnation (2 Cor 3:7,9). The gospel of Jesus Christ is different, it grants believers life, righteousness and freedom (2 Cor 3:6.17).

The new covenant has an eschatological character. It is already now determined by the new spirit which is promised for the end of time.[77] Thus the new covenant – following the promise of a new covenant Jer 31:31–34 and the institution of the Lord's Supper (1 Cor 11:25) – appears before the horizon of the Kingdom of God (Mk 14:25) and the Second Coming of Christ (1 Cor 11:26). It is already part of the new creation, thus making the Sinai covenant part of the present, evil world (Gal 1:4). This new covenant serves the ministry of reconciliation which Paul claims for his own apostolate and the proclamation of the gospel of the reconciling death of Jesus Christ on the

---

[77] Cf. 2 Cor 3:6,17f. with Ez 11:19; 36:26f.; Joel 3:1–5; Acts 2:17–21 (Pentecost).

cross (2 Cor 5:18–21). Humans are brought into this covenant by faith and through baptism and the Lord's Supper; thus they become a new creation in the power of the Holy Spirit:

> "So if anyone is in Christ, there is a new creation: everything old has passed away; see, everything has become new!" (2 Cor 5:17; Gal 6:15; cf. Rev 21:5).

2.2.6 The covenant theology of the Letter to the Hebrews

The author of the Letter to the Hebrews, who is using a different argumentation and addressing the context of a different target group, goes one step further. He explains the opposition between the old and the new covenant by contrasting the order of the Levitical cult with the high priesthood of Christ.

Jesus is the mediator (Heb 8:6; 9:15; 12:24) of a new (9:15; 12:24) and better covenant (7:22; 8:6), which has made "the first one" (8:7,13; 9:1,15,18) obsolete (8:13). The defect of the first covenant was that the sacrificial ministry, offered over and over again, was not able to take away sins (9:25; 10:4,11), whereas Christ as high priest once for all (7:27; 9:12; 10:10) effected eternal redemption (9:12,15) and forgiveness (9:22; 10:18) by his atoning death (2:17) and opened the way to God into the heavenly sanctuary (7:22–25; 10:19).

The fact that the first covenant is outdated is not a criticism of Israel as the chosen people of God, but rather of the previous ritual order, which here represents an example for *every* kind of ritual order which is worldly and temporal (9:10). The new covenant not only replaces the old cult chronologically (8:7,13; 10:9). Rather, they are to be understood as the relationship between pattern and shadow (8:5; 10:1), one being heavenly and eternal and the other earthly and perishable. In the Letter to the Hebrews, the change of priesthood (7:12,18 f.) does not mean that God's people have been supplanted. In his atoning death, Jesus Christ as the true high priest has once and for all provided access to the heavenly sanctuary, which was already predicted to Abraham with the Promised Land and which the "cloud of witnesses" (Heb 12:1) had believed in. Therefore the believers of Old Testament times hope together with the Christian church for the same promise and go towards the same fulfilment (11:39 f. "not apart from us"; 12:22 f.).

Thus the author of the Letter to the Hebrews has managed to transform the motif of the covenant in a Christological, soteriological fashion. The old ritual order is replaced by the soteriological bond to the atoning death and heavenly exaltation of Jesus Christ, whereby atonement is realised once and for all (Heb 9:12; 25 f.; 10:14).

Because the believers of the old and the new covenant are under the same promise, the innovation of the new covenant in Christ can be understood and accepted theologically, without anti-Judaistic tendencies. Of course, this cannot eliminate the clear distinction between the Jewish and the Christian hope for salvation, as seen from the Jewish point of view and brought to bear in the dialogue. The confession of Christ, on the other hand, is the indispensable centre of the Christian faith. Christians can and should express this centre without devaluing the people of Israel, who were first called by God.

2.2.7 Consequences for the celebration of the Lord's Supper and the preparation of sermons

Since the duality of the old and new covenants has been particularly prone to provoke anti-Jewish tendencies in the history of its interpretation and effect, special care is required here when preparing the form of the service, whether in the language of the sermon, the choice of prayers or the selection of hymns. The greatest importance is attached to the reports on the Lord's Supper, which serve as the sermon text on Holy (Maundy) Thursday (Matt. 26:17–30; 1 Cor 11:[17–22],23–26,[27–29, 33–34a]). Otherwise, among the ordinary sermon texts in the lectionary of the German Evangelical churches there are only passages concerning the new covenant (Jer 31:31; 2 Cor 3:6; Heb 12:24); the concept of the old or first covenant appears in the readings 2 Cor 3:14 and Heb 9:15.[78] As has been shown, reference to the

---

[78] Cf. the suggested sermon texts in the new lectionary (cf. editors' preface, p. 8): Jer 31:31-34 (Christmas Eve Vespers OT reading (promises), series I; 6th Sunday after Easter – Exaudi OT II); Mt 26:17-30 (Maundy Thursday sermon text, III); Rom 9:1-5 (10th Sunday after Trinity – Church and Israel epistle reading, II); Rom 11:25-32 (10th Sunday after Trinity – Destruction of Jerusalem epistle reading, II); 1 Cor 11:(17-22)23-26(27-29, 33-34a) (Maundy Thursday epistle reading, I); 2 Cor 3:3-6(7-9) (20th Sunday after Trinity epistle reading, VI); Eph 2:(11-16)17-22 (2nd Sunday after Trinity epistle reading, II/V); Hebr 12:12-18 (19-21), 22-25a (2nd Sunday after Epiphany sermon text, II. Sunday after Epiphany sermon text, VI) as well as further texts outside the sermon series Ex 24:1-11 (Maundy Thursday); Mk 14:17-26 (Maundy Thursday); 2 Cor 3:(12-16)17-18 (Pentecost Sunday); Hebr 9:15,26b-28 (Good Friday).

new covenant always raises – at least implicitly – the question concerning the innovations it brings and what makes the previous covenant obsolete.

The expression "new covenant" is, as shown above, not a Christian invention, but is already to be found in Jer 31.31–34 in an Old Testament prophetic text from post-exilic times. Already at this point, the reference to a previous covenant can only mean the covenant of Sinai (Ex 24), which Israel broke through its idolatry in the story of the Golden Calf (Ex 32). The novelty of this new covenant promised in Jer 31 is that God creates a new covenant partner for himself out of Israel and Judah. God makes a new beginning by desisting from remembering the breach of covenant, overcoming that transgression through forgiveness, and establishing a new covenant in which Israel can once again be a partner. It is an act of new creation that fulfils the petition of Ps 51:10 (Ash Wednesday sermon text, series III), "Create in me a clean heart, O God, and put a new and right spirit within me." Since the idea of the new covenant is primarily the formulation of a contrast within the Old Testament, it describes a creative renewal of Israel. When preparing a sermon, it is necessary to reflect hermeneutically on the way the new covenant is spoken of under Old Testament conditions, without immediately preaching about it in a directly Christological way. Therefore, one must first appreciate the contrast between the old and the new covenant, between the breaking of the covenant, forgiveness and a new beginning through God's grace and mercy, within the Old Testament context, i.e. within the history of Israel, before looking ahead to the new covenant in Jesus' words at the Lord's Supper.

In the New Testament the new covenant first appears in the accounts on the Last Supper (Lk 22:20; 1 Cor 11:25). An explicit direct comparison of the new and the old covenant is only found in Paul, while only the author of the Letter to the Hebrews offers a systematic analysis (see above). There is no point at which this duality indicates that the Old Testament is replaced by the New Testament. The Old Testament is not dismissed, but remains as scripture a binding authority as a testimony of God's action and as a basis for argumentation that helps to demonstrate the eschatological innovation of the new covenant in Christ against the background of the Old Testament testimony. Nowhere in the New Testament is the duality equated with the opposition of the old and the new people of God, Jews and Christians, Church and Israel, ecclesia and synagogue.

In the Lord's Supper, the words of institution recall the Sinai covenant (Mt 26:28; Mk 14:24; cf. Ex 24:8) and identify the cup with the new covenant that Jesus established in his blood (Lk 22:20; 1 Cor 11:25; cf. Jer 31:31-34). With the concept of the covenant, Jesus places his death in the context of God's history with Israel. The motif of the blood of the covenant is connected to the covenant of Sinai (Ex 24:8) typologically[79]. However, the

---

[79] In the *typological* interpretation, persons or institutions are understood as prefigurations of what is to come, for example when Paul describes the first Adam as "typos" of the coming, new Adam (= Christ) (Rom 5:14). In the *allegorical* interpretation it is assumed that the biblical texts carry a hidden meaning beyond the one that is visible. Here, too, Paul may serve as an example when he interprets the rock from which water gushes forth (Ex 17:6), a life-giving rock that followed the children of Israel, as Christ himself (1 Cor 10:4). An *eschatological* interpretation refers to fulfilment at the end of time.

pointed reference to the blood of Jesus ("my blood") indicates the antithetical correspondence to another covenant, showing that the covenant of Jesus is a new one. The statement that Jesus shed his blood vicariously "for many" or "for you" describes the significance of this covenant for salvation. It is made "for the forgiveness of sins", as Matthew adds (Mt 26:28). By characterising his covenant as a covenant of forgiveness, Jesus fulfils in Christian understanding what was announced in the promise of Jer 31:31–34: The days of salvation have come, forgiveness is granted, the end times have begun.

The adjective "new" is not just meant in a temporal, chronological sense, but above all eschatologically. It interprets the death of Jesus as a new settlement by God with great eschatological significance, a comprehensive new beginning, the dawn of the final days, the ultimate beginning of salvation. This can already be recognised in the accounts of the Lord's Supper, with the expectation of renewed drinking of the fruit of the vine in the kingdom of God (Mk 14:25, par.) and the Second Coming of Christ (1 Cor 11:26: "until he comes"). Here the sermon on Maundy Thursday, the day on which the Lord's Supper was instituted, or on the 7th Sunday after Trinity (Communion Sunday), can set a focus and interpret the motif of the New Testament in relation to the congregation's own celebration of the Lord's Supper: "for you".

Liturgical texts which make additions to the words of institution[80] should be handled with great care, both theologically and pastorally, because the *verba testamenti* recited in the

---

[80] The obligatory words of institution are found in the orders of service.

liturgy of the Lord's Supper interpret the meal and make it what it is: the meal hosted by Jesus Christ, given for reconciliation.

The Bible consistently refers to the covenant of Sinai as the direct counterpart to the new covenant.[81] When the new and the old covenant are compared with one another in 2 Cor 3 however, as has already been pointed out, this does not concern a chronological sequence (then and now), but rather the soteriological alternative (either/or) in view of death and life, damnation or righteousness with God. It is about the contrast between the ministry of Moses and the apostolate of Paul, between the Torah of Sinai, which condemns and kills, and the Spirit of Christ, who brings life, righteousness and freedom, between law and gospel.[82] The new covenant does not bring a new Torah, but the gospel of the death and resurrection of Jesus, by which Paul, as a minister of the new covenant, carries out the ministry of reconciliation (2 Cor 3:6; 4:1, 3 f.; 5:14–21).

In this comparison Paul is not concerned with anti-Jewish polemics, but much more fundamentally with a theological critique of the law, to be more precise, of its soteriological inability to bring justification and life. For Paul, the law is indeed in and of itself spiritual, holy, just and good and "promised life" (Rom 7:10-14), but it lacks the power and ability (Rom 8:3) to make alive, as the irrealis mode in Gal 3:21 shows: "For if a law *had been given* that *could* make alive, then righteousness *would* indeed *come* through the law." But because the law does

---

[81] Jer 31:31–34; Mk 14:24; Mt 26:28; 2 Cor 3:6,14; Gal 4:24; cf. 3:15–18.

[82] Cf. the same contrast between the Sinai Torah and the promise to Abraham in Gal 3:6–4:31.

not have this life-creating power, its ministry proves to be a ministry that kills (2 Cor 3:6f.).

Paul's critique is not aimed at a specific Jewish point of view, but much more fundamentally at a basic anthropological condition. Therefore any criticism of the law in the sermon should not take the Jewish Torah as an example, but rather develop the theme on the basis of the "law of sin and of death" (Rom 8:2), i. e. the laws and rules, principles and norms, constraints and structures of this unredeemed world (Gal 1:4). Paul warns not only against the bondage under the Torah of Sinai (Gal 4:24f.; 5:1), but also of the bondage "under the elements of the world",[83] i.e. under the weak and wretched powers of this world, which in truth are not gods (4:3,8f.). He contrasts them with the liberating effect of the Spirit of God:

"For the law of the Spirit of life in Christ Jesus has set you free from the law of sin and of death." (Rom 8:2; cf. 2 Cor 3:6,17)

Here it is necessary nowadays to think further about the potential of Paul's critique of the law when it comes to an ideological assessment of the regulations and norms, claims to rule and structures of power, and the systemic or factual constraints of this world. The consequential, fatal experiences of disaster, powerlessness and suffering awaken a longing for liberation and redemption.[84] The presentation of this gospel continues to

---

[83] The New Revised Standard Version translates "enslaved to the elemental spirits of the world".

[84] Cf. section 1 of this manual (Human existence before God: law and gospel), especially 1.2.4 g.

be the real commission of theology and proclamation, exegesis, preaching and teaching. This can not only ensure that anti-Jewish associations are avoided; above all the Pauline concept of law in its anthropological and existential relevance is made fruitful for today's distinction between law and gospel, so that the liberating message of Jesus Christ is brought to the fore. In a similar way, one can deal with the Letter to the Hebrews and its criticism of the Levitical priesthood, which serves as a representative model for every worldly and perishable ritual order on earth (Heb 9:10).

Closely connected to the question of the old and new covenant is also the last topic we are going to examine.

2.3 The distinction between promise and fulfilment[85]

2.3.1 Introductory remarks

The double expression promise and fulfilment is not only to be found in worship services, liturgical practice and hymnals, but also corresponds to a widespread understanding: the Old Testament offers promises or prophecies that have been fulfilled in Christ.

This connection becomes especially clear during the period of Advent and at Christmas, when texts from the book of Isaiah (especially the so-called Messianic promises in Isa 7:14; 9:1–6

---

[85] Cf. Uwe Becker, Verheißung und Erfüllung. Zu einem Grundmodell der christlichen Rezeption der jüdischen Bibel, in: Die lutherischen Duale (see note 6), pp. 233–254.

and 11:1-9) are read and sung, foreshadowing their final fulfil-ment:

> "The people who in darkness walked / have seen a glorious light; the heav'nly dawn broke forth on those / who dwelt in death and night." (John Morison, 1781)

In historical-critical biblical scholarship, this complementary pair of terms hardly comes into play as a category of interpretation. It is only of limited use for the scientific, exegetical approach to the Bible. On the other hand, it has often proved valuable when dealing with biblical texts for theological and religious purposes. Within the Bible itself, this connection is already made in the New Testament in order to establish intertextual references[86] and to understand the events of Christ against the background of the Old Testament and the promise of God for Israel to which it bears witness. In later times, the figure of promise and fulfilment often played a prominent role in the Church's interpretation of scripture. From the outset it was a central category for the Christian interpretation of the Old Testament, that is to say, in the light of the testimony to Christ.

---

[86] Intertextuality describes the way in which a text is read in relation to other texts, so that new connotations are constantly created – within the Bible, for example, between different biblical books and texts. The interaction of various texts suggested for church worship and the liturgical year also gives rise to new connotations and associations. Cf. section 2.1 of this manual (The distinction between faith and works), especially 2.1.4.

The duality of promise and fulfilment is helpful for the creative theological development of biblical texts and intertextualities, especially where they are clearly appropriate to the combination of readings and sermon texts offered by the lectionary.

The reference to this duality in the history of interpretation, whether in New Testament times or in ecclesiastical and theological tradition, can still be an inspiration for sermons today. However, misinterpretations and misunderstandings have to be ruled out, especially those that lead to a defamation and devaluation of Judaism. That was not infrequently the case in the past, and can still happen today.

So it would be quite wrong to reduce the Old Testament as a whole to the function of a *promise* that had been *fulfilled* in the New Testament and thus done with. In fact, there is an *overhang* of unfulfilled promises in both Testaments, coupled with the hope of their fulfilment by God. It would be just as wrong to use the conviction that the New Testament had fulfilled the Old Testament promises in order to criticise or even reject other interpretations of such promises, especially in the Jewish tradition of interpretation.

2.3.2 Use of the two terms

In early Christianity the pattern of promise and fulfilment was used to interpret the scriptures as a foreshadowing of God's redemptive act in Jesus Christ. It was not only applied to individual Old Testament promises, but also to the Bible as a whole. Thus, as a hermeneutical method, this pattern is on an equal footing with *allegorical* and *typological* interpretation.[87]

---

[87] Cf. note 79.

In the New Testament all these models of interpretation are already used in order to show that the Old Testament scriptures *should in fact* be read with reference to Christ; they explain the story of Christ in the context of God's promises and testify to the fact that they had been finally realised. Using this explanation, the New Testament reads and interprets the Old Testament – the scriptures of that time – from the point of view of, and looking towards, the gospel of Christ.[88] That is, the New Testament itself gives us an insight into an inner-Jewish dispute about the interpretation of "the scriptures". This is an example and precursor of the attitude that determines the interpretation of the Old Testament up to the present: that there is a Jewish interpretation of the Old Testament, of various kinds, and a varied interpretation of the Old Testament in the Christian community, which – following the authors of the New Testament – hears and receives the Old Testament in the light of the proclamation of Christ.

In essence, it is a question of different understandings of scripture: that of the Jewish and that of the Christian interpretation of the Old Testament tradition. According to the perspective of Christian reading it is always clear: It is only one's own conviction of faith which can reveal the real character of the Old Testament texts in its deep meaning as a promise. This takes place retrospectively, i.e. in the light of the belief in their fulfilment in the coming of Christ.

---

[88] Cf. alone the argumentation of this kind quoted in the sermons or confessions in Acts, for example by Peter, Stephen, Philip and Paul (Acts 2:16,25,31,34; 3:22,25; 7, passim; 8:35; 9:22 etc.).

2.3.3 The duality as a method of Early Christian scriptural interpretation

The New Testament makes use of the interpretative pattern of promise and fulfilment in many ways. It does not only make use of isolated Old Testament texts like the prophecies in Isaiah, but it also takes the scriptures as a whole. Thus we encounter characteristic phrases like "so it has been written", "to fulfil what had been spoken" / "to let the scriptures be fulfilled" and "in accordance with the scriptures".[89] A particularly striking example of the reference to concrete individual texts are the so-called fulfilment quotations in Matthew (cf. Mt 1:23, quoting Isa 7:14).

From a *historical* perspective, the Old Testament texts have a meaning of their own – for example, the expectation of a renewed kingship from the house of David. From the perspective of modern scientific exegesis of the Old Testament, as such, the citations of fulfilment in the New Testament and the implied hermeneutical procedure of verification and fulfilment are no longer incontrovertibly applicable, as long as they do not correspond to this (re-)constructed original meaning of the Old Testament texts in historical criticism. They formulate a connection that transcends the original sense of the Old Testament texts understood in this way and, moreover, they risk degrading them to a mere precursor of the New Testament.

Nevertheless, one should distinguish between the pattern of interpretation as such and the subject matter addressed with its help in the New Testament texts – from the perspective of

---

[89] For example: Mt 1:22f.; Mk 14:49; Lk 24:44; 1 Cor 15:3f. etc.

faith in Christ and for the sermon. When, for example, the whole of "scripture" is spoken of as having been "fulfilled" in the person and fate of Jesus (e.g. Rom 1:2 and 1 Cor 15:3b-5), the claim is impressively clear that the Old Testament scriptures as a whole testify to God's salvation as witnessed in the New Testament, in order to proclaim the coming of Christ as its fulfilment. Individual regulations such as the ceremonial law are no longer valid, but scripture is understood in its *proper* intention from the perspective of the New Testament texts as a promise of Christ and thus brought to its goal hermeneutically.

2.3.4 Clarifying the terminology

In everyday language the two words *promise* and *prophecy* are not clearly distinguished, yet they convey different nuances: while *prophecy* in a more technical sense refers to a prognosis of future events on the basis of supernatural inspiration, the *promise* as a translation of the Greek *epangelía* or the Latin *promissio* is more closely related to biblical usage (cf. Rom 4:13f.,16f., 20; Gal 3:14–18; Heb 10:36).

This clarification of the term could help to avoid misunderstanding a *promise* as a prognosis which can be proved by the concrete, historically verifiable occurrence and subsequently disregarded. The term indicates rather the character as *promissio*, something which can also prove itself anew in different situations.

If one were to understand individual texts in the sense of a *prophecy,* the duality of promise and fulfilment would thus hardly be suitable to express adequately the Christian interpretation of the Old Testament – particularly from today's perspective. If one understands the concept of promise in the second sense as *promissio*, applying it to the Old Testament as a whole, one is able to express the openness and incompleteness of the first part of the canon without excluding alternative Jewish interpretations *per se*.

2.3.5 This duality in Luther's theology

Unlike the relationship between law and gospel, this is not a genuine topic in Luther's or Lutheran theology. On the contrary, we can observe a particularly broad reception of the scheme of promise and fulfilment in Reformed theology, for example in the covenant theology of Johannes Coccejus or also in Karl Barth.

In his commentaries on the Old Testament, Luther essentially held on to the hermeneutical principles already used in the New Testament, even though he attaches increasing importance to the literal sense[90] and is sometimes also critical of allegorism. His attitude towards the Old Testament as a whole can hardly be reduced to one single factor.

On the one hand, there is no question for Luther that the Old Testament has to be understood as a whole in accordance with the New Testament message of Jesus Christ; this is the starting point and end point. In doing so, he adopts the Pauline view of the gospel of God, "which he promised beforehand through his prophets in the holy scriptures" (Rom 1:2), as a hermeneutical approach to the linkage of the Old and New

---

[90] From the Latin *littera* (letter), meaning the face value or literal meaning of the text; for other levels of meaning in interpretation, see note 79.

Testaments. It is precisely in the duality of promise and fulfilment that this perspective comes into its own. Luther's appre-
ciation of the Old Testament as an indissoluble part of the
Christian canon owes a great deal to this hermeneutic, which
holds on to the unity of the Old and New Testaments in the perspective of the story of Christ.

Against this background, the Old Testament comes to be regarded as a book of God's promises given to the believers in
Old Testament times. For Luther, together with the authors of
the New Testament, they reach their fulfilment in the coming
of Christ.

This hermeneutic of the Old Testament[91] as a promise of
Christ is central to Luther's theology. For example, he understands the prophets as heralds of "Christ's kingdom"; the
messianic promises of the Old Testament are for him of central
importance for the understanding of Christ's mission; he understands Gen 3:15 as the protoevangelium in order to comprehend the whole history of salvation to be based on the gospel;
the "cloud of witnesses", who believed in God's promise according to the reports in the Old Testament, were for Luther already believers in Christ. In this way, the theological intention
of this hermeneutic of the unity of scripture under the duality
of promise and fulfilment emerges: Luther wants to recognise
scripture in its unity as the voice and action of the *one* God who
in Jesus Christ, "the mirror of the Father's heart"[92], has recon-

---

[91] Cf. Reinhard Schwarz, Martin Luther (see note 61), pp. 45–75.

[92] Martin Luther, The Large Catechism (1529), interpretation of the
3rd article of the Apostles' Creed, in: The Book of Concord (see
note 30), p. 440.

ciled the world to himself and grants it participation through faith in the gospel. This hermeneutic, theologically orientated to the gospel, also comes into effect in the duality of promise and fulfilment, and is nevertheless accompanied by a thoroughly differentiated philological and theological approach to the Old Testament.

At the same time, however, Luther, especially in the late phase of his life, allowed himself to indulge in devastating condemnations of the Jews, aberrations which the Lutheran churches and their preachers most emphatically reject and which fill them with shame.

2.3.6 On the current relevance of the duality

In the current discussion, one encounters a criticism of the traditional use of the duality of promise and fulfilment that is both fundamental and severe. This criticism derives from the Christian-Jewish dialogue: the Old Testament is to be set free from its role as a mere predecessor and perceived in its own sense. On the one hand, this criticism immediately stands to reason, because the texts of the Hebrew Bible have been interpreted in Judaism independently and in many different ways. On the other hand, the Old Testament was and is understood in the Christian Church against the background of Christ's coming. Thus there is a twofold historical effect, which is reflected in the thesis of the "twofold conclusion of the Old Testament in Judaism and Christianity".[93]

---

[93] Klaus Koch, Der doppelte Ausgang des Alten Testaments in Judentum und Christentum, in: JBTh 6/1991, pp. 215–242; similarly

We must therefore seriously assume that first generation Christians put the new eschatological experience into words by describing the mission of Christ as a fulfilment, indeed *the* fulfilment, of certain Old Testament texts with which they were generally familiar word for word. This does not mean, however, that they claimed the exclusive application of the texts in this way, and that there is no longer any potential of promise (cf. Rom 8:11) pointing beyond the events that are testified to in the New Testament. It is rather the case that the hope in God's future action, which makes a new creation and opens up new possibilities, is kept alive. Hope in what is promised and not seen is crucial to faith (Heb 11:1).

2.3.7 Consequences for sermon preparation

The exegesis of the biblical texts leads to the conclusion that the promises in the Old Testament concerning a figure who is later to appear (e.g. the Advent and Christmas texts Isa 7:14; 9:1-6 or 11:1-9) do not testify to God's redemptive work in Christ by a historically exaggerated inner meaning. They can, however, serve to illustrate the salvation testified to in the New Testament, e.g. by relating the readings during the service and the explanations in the sermon to one another. In this way, the hope of salvation of both Jews and Christians can be included

---

also the Catholic Old Testament scholar Gross (Walter Gross, Der doppelte Ausgang der Bibel Israels und die doppelte Leseweise des christlichen Alten Testaments, in: ibid. (ed.), Das Judentum. Eine bleibende Herausforderung christlicher Identität, Mainz 2001, pp. 9-25).

in a fruitful exchange. That the Old Testament texts are included in the lectionary order for the Sundays in question already indicates how church congregations use this duality in worship; in the horizon of the gospel, it relates the texts of the Old Testament to the events around Christ, hearing and receiving them in the context of the Christian church services.

3 Conclusion: The importance of Lutheran dualities

It should now be clear that the dualities discussed here are not a burden, but an achievement of Lutheran theology in particular and of the confessions in the Reformation tradition and the Christian faith in general. They are an effective antidote against a biblicism that equates the loyalty to scripture with a commitment to every single statement within it. They formulate an aid to understanding the diversity of biblical texts in the unity of the Old and New Testaments by bringing the gospel of Jesus of Nazareth to the fore.

The Reformation theologians did not overlook the diversity of the scriptures and their statements, and they also took those texts seriously which do not directly express the gospel of Jesus Christ. Precisely for that reason, in order to perceive the unity of scripture, they resorted to dualities which either complement or contradict one another:

Law and gospel: Thus, the texts on the gospel of God's unconditional grace correspond to those that the sinner can only understand and experience as judgement. These demanding texts also point to Christ by convicting the sinner of sin and pointing to Christ as the basis of salvation. By contradicting the gospel, the law constitutes a witness *to* the gospel.

Faith and works: Texts on the gospel of justification by faith alone correspond to those that demand ethical commitment from human beings – but only under the premise that human beings are not justified before God of their own accord, by their positive or negative qualities or achievements, but through the gospel of Jesus Christ. These texts are understood in such a way that they speak of attentiveness to one's neighbour and to the world, which becomes possible in every kind of way, as long as one is freed from concern for oneself and is moved by the love of God with which he first loved humans.

Old and new covenant: The church understands itself as the fellowship of the new covenant established by Jesus Christ and takes the history of God with his chosen people Israel seriously. For just this reason it associates this history of God's action with the people of Israel with its own experience of God, revealed to it in the encounter with the person and work of Jesus Christ. It understands the new covenant established by the cross and resurrection of Jesus Christ for the reconciliation of the world as the action of God, by which he leads those who believe in Christ into communion with himself.

Promise and fulfilment: The duality of promise and fulfilment brings a theological concept into play in the context of the *Christian* treatment of the Bible. This holds that the scriptures bear witness to the voice and action of the *one* God who in Jesus Christ has realised his unconditional will of salvation towards the world once and for all, in which all can partake who believe in Jesus Christ.

All in all, Paul's "theology of Israel" from his later period (Rom 9–11) draws attention to the fact that, notwithstanding the conviction that salvation for all people is only possible through Christ, the existence of a people of God that does not believe in Christ is a reality. This situation is not only tolerated by God but also foreseen in his plan of salvation for the benefit of the Gentile believers. It is unimportant whether one agrees with all the statements of Paul in detail. What is decisive is that Israel remains uninterruptedly the object of God's election and love.

Common to all these dualities is that there is no question of a substitution of Israel or Jewishness and no denial of God's love for his people. This becomes clear when one takes the following two aspects into account: first of all, the dualities show a clear reference to existence; beyond that, they thematise a self-understanding that proves to be effected by studying the biblical texts. This applies most clearly to the dualities law and gospel as well as faith and works, but also to the dualities old and new covenant as well as promise and fulfilment, which are terminologically more strongly influenced by the history of salvation.

It is a separate and indispensable hermeneutical step to become aware of the fact that in general the dualities describe or cause possibilities of human existence – thus describing a "legalism" that unites Jews, Christians, Muslims and followers of non-religious world views. The gospel of justification by faith in Christ is the contrary term, the invitation to the antidote, effective both for Christians and non-Christians. For preachers it is a special challenge to present the Lutheran description of general human possibilities of existence in such a way that they illuminate the different experiences of oneself and the world – whether those of "religiously musical" people or those of people who understand themselves to be secularly minded – and to make them aware of the liberating power of the gospel for their own specific life.

All these dualities are guided by the conviction that salvation is to be found in Christ. Therefore they direct their understanding of God's action towards this central belief, while emphasising precisely the fact that all people, Jews and non-Jews, are destined to become partakers of this salvation, and that all people tend to resist this salvation.

In this respect, the dualities do not simply have a function for the exegetical understanding of scripture as a text, but they lead to an understanding of human beings and their world by means of scripture. The dualities help to open up human existence and lead us to understand it as "God's concern".

The explanations in this manual should describe how an interpretation of scripture on the basis of these dualities, and thus on the gospel of Christ, can be implemented in preaching practice – with care, and staying close to the phenomena of human existence. Such preaching, guided by these dualities, can do justice to the diversity of scripture and the diversity of human life situations. The dualities serve to lead to an understanding of God, of oneself and the world that is revealed by the gospel of Jesus Christ.

Appendix

Members of the VELKD Commission on Theology 2015–2021

Prof. Dr. Dr. h. c. Christine Axt-Piscalar, Chair of Systematic Theology, Göttingen (Chair)

Prof. Dr. Notger Slenczka, Chair of Systematic Theology, Berlin (Deputy Chair)

Prof. Dr. Uwe Becker, Chair of Old Testament, Jena

OKR Prof. Dr. Ulrich Heckel, Evangelical Church of Württemberg, Stuttgart

Prof. Dr. Michael Herbst, Chair of Practical Theology, Greifswald

Prof. Dr. Rochus Leonhardt, Institute for Systematic Theology, Leipzig

Regional Bishop Prof. Dr. Stefan Ark Nitsche, Nuremberg

Prof. Dr. Ilona Nord, Institute for Protestant Theology and Religious Education, Würzburg

Dr. Renate Penßel, Institute for Church Law, Erlangen

Prof. Dr. Wolf-Friedrich Schäufele, Department of Church History, Marburg

Senior Pastor and Provost Dr. Martin Vetter, Church District Hamburg-East

Prof. Dr. Achim Behrens, Lutheran Theological University, Oberursel (Guest from Independent Evangelical-Lutheran Church)

OKR Dr. Martin Evang, Department of the United Evangelical Church (UEK) in the Church Office of the EKD (guest from UEK)

OKR Dr. Martin Hauger, Church Office of the EKD (guest from EKD)

OKR Dr. Claas Cordemann, formerly in the Department of the United Evangelical Lutheran Church of Germany (VELKD) in the Church Office of the EKD (Secretary 2016–2018)

OKR Dr. Andreas Ohlemacher, Department of the United Evangelical Lutheran Church of Germany (VELKD) in the Church Office of the EKD (Secretary since 2018)

Florian Hübner
Henrike Müller (Eds.)

What is Lutheran?

Introductions to
Theology, Worship,
Congregation, Ecumenism
and Church Law

*Lutheran Theology: German
Perspectives and Positions | 1*

208 pages | paperback
12 x 19 cm
ISBN 978-3-374-05913-3
EUR 20,00 [D]

In the 21st century, Lutheran theology takes place on a global level. Just as the Lutheran communion has spread into all parts of the world, so also theology is now practised in a variety of linguistic and cultural contexts. For this reason, the United Evangelical Lutheran Church of Germany (VELKD), in cooperation with the German National Committee of the Lutheran World Federation, is starting a series of English translations of current VELKD publications.

The first volume contains five texts by well-known German theologians on core topics of the Lutheran Church: Theology (Michael Roth), Worship (Christian Lehnert), Congregations (Martin Kumlehn), Ecumenism (Bernd Oberdorfer) and Church Law (Hendrik Munsonius).

EVANGELISCHE VERLAGSANSTALT
Leipzig www.eva-leipzig.de

Tel +49 (0) 341/ 7 11 41 -44   shop@eva-leipzig.de

Bilateral Working Group
of the German Bishops'
Conference and the United
Evangelical Lutheran
Church of Germany (Ed.)

**God and the Dignity
of Humans**

*Lutheran Theology: German
Perspectives and Positions | 2*

192 pages | paperback
12 x 19 cm
ISBN 978-3-374-06430-4
EUR 18,00 [D]

Is it possible for the churches to take a joint stand on human dignity, even though they hold different positions in certain ethical questions? This study paper by the (Roman Catholic) German Bishops' Conference and the United Evangelical Lutheran Church of Germany, which is available in English for the first time, explores new paths in the ecumenical handling of ethical questions. Using the methodology of "differentiated consensus", the authors outline the theological similarities of the churches' teaching of anthropology, whilst still doing justice to their differences in the ethical assessment of individual issues of human conduct. In this way, Catholics and Lutherans adopt a common position and make a theologically responsible contribution to ethical judgement.

EVANGELISCHE VERLAGSANSTALT
Leipzig   www.eva-leipzig.de

Tel +49 (0) 341/ 7 11 41 -44   shop@eva-leipzig.de

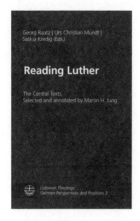

Georg Raatz | Urs Christian Mundt | Saskia Kredig (Eds.)

Reading Luther

The Central Texts. Selected and annotated by Martin H. Jung

Lutheran Theology: German Perspectives and Positions | 3

296 pages | paperback
12 x 19 cm
ISBN 978-3-374-06940-8
EUR 20,00 [D]

Take a fresh look at Martin Luther and his original works! Here the fundamental key texts have been compiled in one single book, introduced by Martin H. Jung's informative commentaries. The English language translations are up to date and easily understood. Apart from well-known works such as the »95 Theses« and »On the Freedom of a Christian«, this collection also contains dogmatic and devotional texts as well as problematic tracts, for example on the Turks and the Jews. They provide an easily readable insight into the authentic Luther. The book is well suited for confirmation classes, youth groups and adult education as well as for use in churches, congregations, schools and institutions. The book is strongly to be recommended not just for study purposes but also for private reading.

EVANGELISCHE VERLAGSANSTALT
Leipzig www.eva-leipzig.de

Tel +49 (0) 341/ 7 11 41 -44   shop@eva-leipzig.de